Grammatical Inference for Computational Linguistics

Synthesis Lectures on Human Language Technologies

Editor
Graeme Hirst, *University of Toronto*

Synthesis Lectures on Human Language Technologies is edited by Graeme Hirst of the University of Toronto. The series consists of 50- to 150-page monographs on topics relating to natural language processing, computational linguistics, information retrieval, and spoken language understanding. Emphasis is on important new techniques, on new applications, and on topics that combine two or more HLT subfields.

Grammatical Inference for Computational Linguistics
Jeffrey Heinz, Colin de la Higuera, and Menno van Zaanen
2015

Automatic Detection of Verbal Deception
Eileen Fitzpatrick, Joan Bachenko, and Tommaso Fornaciari
2015

Natural Language Processing for Social Media
Atefeh Farzindar and Diana Inkpen
2015

Semantic Similarity from Natural Language and Ontology Analysis
Sébastien Harispe, Sylvie Ranwez, Stefan Janaqi, and Jacky Montmain
2015

Learning to Rank for Information Retrieval and Natural Language Processing, Second Edition
Hang Li
2014

Ontology-Based Interpretation of Natural Language
Philipp Cimiano, Christina Unger, and John McCrae
2014

Automated Grammatical Error Detection for Language Learners, Second Edition
Claudia Leacock, Martin Chodorow, Michael Gamon, and Joel Tetreault
2014

Grammatical Inference for Computational Linguistics

Jeffrey Heinz, Colin de la Higuera, Menno van Zaanen

ISBN: 978-3-031-01031-6   paperback
ISBN: 978-3-031-02159-6   ebook

DOI: 10.1007/978-3-031-02159-6

 A Publication in the Springer Nature series
SYNTHESIS LECTURES ONADVANCES IN AUTOMOTIVE TECHNOLOGY
Series ISSN: 1947-4040 print   1947-4059 ebook

Lecture #28
Series Editor: Graeme Hirst, *University of Toronto*

First Edition
10 9 8 7 6 5 4 3 2 1

Grammatical Inference for Computational Linguistics

Jeffrey Heinz
University of Delaware

Colin de la Higuera
Nantes University

Menno van Zaanen
Tilburg University

SYNTHESIS LECTURES ON HUMAN LANGUAGE TECHNOLOGIES #28

ABSTRACT

This book provides a thorough introduction to the subfield of theoretical computer science known as grammatical inference from a computational linguistic perspective. Grammatical inference provides principled methods for developing computationally sound algorithms that learn structure from strings of symbols. The relationship to computational linguistics is natural because many research problems in computational linguistics are learning problems on words, phrases, and sentences: What algorithm can take as input some finite amount of data (for instance a corpus, annotated or otherwise) and output a system that behaves "correctly" on specific tasks?

Throughout the text, the key concepts of grammatical inference are interleaved with illustrative examples drawn from problems in computational linguistics. Special attention is paid to the notion of "learning bias." In the context of computational linguistics, such bias can be thought to reflect common (ideally universal) properties of natural languages. This bias can be incorporated either by identifying a learnable class of languages which contains the language to be learned or by using particular strategies for optimizing parameter values. Examples are drawn largely from two linguistic domains (phonology and syntax) which span major regions of the Chomsky Hierarchy (from regular to context-sensitive classes). The conclusion summarizes the major lessons and open questions that grammatical inference brings to computational linguistics.

KEYWORDS

grammatical inference, language learning, natural languages, formal languages

To our families, friends, and automata

Contents

List of Figures

List of Tables

Preface

Once authors have written the words "The End," they realize how much has been left out. And this rule holds if instead of one author, there are three. This is one reason why prefaces are important. They let readers know (and remind the authors) what the book achieves and what it does not.

The tasks addressed in this book become more formidable with each passing day. It is becoming more complex and intricate because there are more and more cases where one is delivered a huge amount of strings, words, or sentences, or has access to some such data, and one is asked how to build a model summarizing or explaining this information. Furthermore, for many reasons— for example, the fact that most computer scientists have taken courses on graph theory and formal languages—the types of models people are seeking will be very often linked with grammars and automata.

That is why, today, there are people attempting to build or infer grammars or finite-state machines in fields as different as verification, pattern recognition, bioinformatics, and linguistics. That is why techniques of all sorts are being used to infer these models: some rely on statistics, others on linear algebra, some on formal language theory, and many quite often on a combination of these. And finally, that is why certain choices have been made in this book, and therefore some readers might be frustrated.

Before we explain why some of our choices may frustrate readers, let us state who we think our readers are. One reason we embarked on this project was because there is no text which introduces grammatical inference to people working in computational linguistics and natural language processing. Our hope is that this book helps bridge the gap between the needs of *these* researchers and a particular way of thinking about the problems of learning automata and grammars in machine learning. We sincerely believe grammatical inference can help address problems in computational linguistics and that problems in computational linguistics can inform and lead to new developments in grammatical inference (in fact, such mutual benefits exist and are ongoing).

We also have in mind readers who are not encountering automata and grammars for the first time. The kind of background knowledge we expect readers to have is of the type that could be found in standard textbooks on formal language theory that one might take as an advanced undergraduate student or a beginning graduate student. We also expect readers to have some familiarity with topics in computational linguistics and natural language processing, like the kinds discussed in the books by Jurafsky and Martin [2008] or Manning and Schütze [1999] (or their more recent editions).

So what are the choices that may frustrate readers? The first choice we made was to concentrate on *only some* tools and techniques, and not attempt to be exhaustive.

The second choice was to cover the tools and techniques which have been developed in what may informally be called the school of grammatical inference, as represented, over the past 30 years, by the papers published in the series of conferences called ICGI—International Conference on Grammatical Inference. These share a certain number of aspects.

- They build upon well-understood formal language formalisms and avoid, whenever possible, technical complications in the definitions of the objects themselves.

- They either attempt to deliver formal learnability results, independent of some particular corpus, or, on the other hand, aim to produce a very general algorithm whose proof of concept will be given by its results on particular corpora without corpus-specific tweaks.

Consequently, this means the knowledge we present builds from formal language theory and concentrates on those techniques whose intricate theoretical backbone comes from that field.

A third choice is that the book is not self-contained, in the sense that not every algorithm discussed is presented and proved correct in full detail. Instead, we have chosen to focus on ideas, and to include only the notation, definitions, and theorems that we felt important because they support those main points. We do not include proofs, but we try to point to them and further material which helps readers find detailed descriptions and explanations of the algorithms or formalisms. For instance, we often refer to de la Higuera [2010], a book on grammatical inference with a general orientation, which is self-contained.

Together all of this means leaving out certain results, which no doubt deserve closer attention.

For finite-state machines, one notable area left out is *spectral methods*, which identify finite-state machines with sets of matrices and therefore transforms the learning problem into one which searches for an optimal set of parameters which fits those matrices. The techniques here are attractive: they allow the learning of very rich classes of finite-state machines, rely on linear algebra's vast literature, and can be redefined as global optimization problems, for which a large number of researchers are bettering the algorithms all the time.

For formal grammars, a number of results (sometimes grouped under the name *grammar induction*) are based on starting with a backbone grammar, either extremely general or devised from using data for which the structure is known, and adjusting the parameters by just observing relative frequencies. The types of grammars will themselves be adapted to better fit the knowledge we have of natural language.

We do not argue here that the techniques covered in this book work better, just that they correspond to a uniform set of ideas which, when understood, can allow a number of problems to be solved.

Perhaps one argument which we would like to put forward is that of intelligibility. Albeit informal in most cases, the idea is that the types of techniques proposed in this book rely on wanting to understand the machines and grammars learned. An undeclared goal is that one should be able to run a grammatical inference algorithm, obtain perhaps a large automaton or grammar, and nevertheless be able to observe it and understand it, not just its effects. This helps to explain why we believe that the issue of learning the *structure* of the grammar is essential, and why this theme recurs throughout the book.

One may wonder if this is necessary, as the grammar will often be evaluated through a success or error rate, not through its capacity to speak to us. On the other hand, there are increasingly many applications where the user wants more than a black box.

All of this, and the idea of making the book useful to as many readers as possible, was what the authors had in mind when they launched this adventure.

ACKNOWLEDGMENTS

The authors would like to thank Dion Bot, Rémi Eyraud, Thomas Graf, Ákos Kádár, Esmée Mertens, Jim Rogers, Eva Ummelen, Merel van de Wiel, and the anonymous reviewers for their useful feedback.

Jeffrey Heinz gladly thanks Mika, Emma, and Maya for their support.

Colin de la Higuera is grateful to Lindsey for her support.

Menno van Zaanen would like to thank Tanja, Colwin, and Lejla for their support.

September 2015

CHAPTER 1

Studying Learning

Grammatical inference is a subfield of theoretical computer science which aims to characterize, understand, and solve learning problems in terms of formal languages and grammars. The field of computational linguistics faces many different kinds of tasks which involve *natural* languages and learning. Many of these tasks aim to automate decisions and processes that humans accurately undertake every day with apparently very little conscious effort. Examples include word recognition and segmentation, the phonological, morphological, syntactic, semantic, and pragmatic analysis of both speech and written texts, and, at least for multilingual speakers, translation.

Computationally, these are difficult problems, each with their own subproblems and subtleties, but there can be little doubt that solving nearly every one of them goes hand-in-hand with understanding natural language systems. Natural languages are *systems* with their own internal logics, rules, constraints, and structures. It is one of the grand mysteries of contemporary times that humans appear to have this knowledge (as evidenced by their mostly uniform behavior in many linguistic tasks) despite the fact that it is *unconscious* (humans cannot easily articulate it in any detail) and *untaught* (while it is acquired it is not explicitly taught). In fact, it is one of the goals of the academic disciplines of theoretical and descriptive linguistics to precisely state the types of systems natural languages are.

The grand mystery may be solved by one of the marvelous promises of modern times. The development of hardware and software that can make discoveries and learn has changed—and continues to change—our society and our lives. If the systems that underly natural languages can be learned by such machines and programs—if these logics, rules, constraints, and structures can be automatically acquired—then virtually all of the above tasks will be solvable automatically by machines.

Grammatical inference goes to the heart of this enterprise. The "grammar" in "grammatical inference" refers to any aspect of the logics, rules, constraints, and structures that compose the systems underlying natural language. Grammars are models of these systems of knowledge. "Inference" refers to rational steps made in acquiring knowledge from observations and prior assumptions about those observations. At its core, grammatical inference is a method of inquiry that tries to understand the computations involved in making inferences about grammars from observations under a variety of different learning scenarios.

The purpose of this book is to introduce computational linguists to the major results of this field and to its way of thinking. While the field of grammatical inference has much to offer computational linguistics, there is no doubt that computational linguists can make contributions to the field of grammatical inference as well.

The notion of grammar adopted here is broad enough that it can be used for any generative system, including non-linguistic ones in other fields. For example, there can be grammars for DNA or RNA sequences, for the order in which messages should be sent over a computer network, or for the structure of web pages. In this book, however, we will either discuss situations that deal with natural language data or discuss topics that are of general nature (and hence valid for all types of data).

1.1   AN OVERVIEW OF GRAMMATICAL INFERENCE

Grammatical inference takes a cue from formal language theory. Knowledge regarding a natural language can be modeled with a formal language. For instance, the knowledge of which sentences in a natural language are well formed can be modeled with a formal language that contains all and only those sequences of words which together constitute the set of well-formed sentences. Another example comes from phonology: the fact that English speakers generally can (and do and will) coin words like "bling" but generally cannot (and do not and will not) coin words like "gding" can be modeled with a formal language that contains all and only those sequences of letters (or phonemes or speech sounds) which make up the possible well-formed words of the language. While these sets of sentences and words are infinite, grammars are finite representations of these formal languages. Henceforth, we will refer to the elements of formal languages—these sequences of symbols—as strings.

While these examples are simple, more complex knowledge can also be modeled with formal languages. If well-formedness is stochastic, then probabilistic grammars can be used. If syntactic constituency is part of the knowledge we wish to model, then we can introduce symbols into the strings which represent constituent boundary symbols. Whether these abstract symbols are observable to learners depends on the learning scenario. Since practically anything can be represented with strings (even a video, even a grammar), the use of formal language theory is sufficiently broad for the form of inquiry undertaken by researchers in grammatical inference.

Grammatical inference construes the learning process broadly as follows. The setup is shown in Figure 1.1. Information from the language that is to be learned is provided by an abstract entity called the *oracle*. The oracle has access to a grammar, description, representation, or model of the

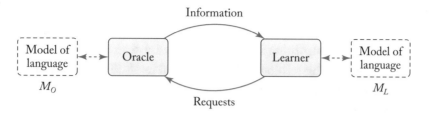

FIGURE 1.1: General overview of the process of grammatical inference.

language (M_O). Based on this knowledge, the oracle can provide learners with information, which typically consists of strings that are valid according to model M_O. The task of the *learner* is now to create its own model (M_L) of the language based on the information (that comes from the model M_O) provided by the oracle. The learner may make requests to the oracle for information.

Within this general framework, several concrete decisions need to be made to establish a precise learning scenario. What kind of information does the oracle provide the learner? What kind of requests can the learner make, if any? How close does M_L have to be to M_O to count as successful learning?

Typically, the information provided to the learner by the oracle is in the shape of strings that are part of the language that the model M_O describes (or when the learning scenario allows, explicitly marked as not being part of the language of M_O). There are several ways the learner may ask for additional information. For instance, the learner may simply ask for another string or specifically ask whether a string so far unseen is valid or not. These choices change the specific setting of the learning process. Additionally, whether certain types of information, such as tree structures or semantic features, are allowed or not is also a choice of the particular learning scenario adopted.

1.2   FORMAL AND EMPIRICAL GRAMMATICAL INFERENCE

In this book, we will describe two different approaches to grammatical inference as a science. First, we will discuss *formal* grammatical inference and, second, *empirical* grammatical inference. Roughly speaking, the former addresses *general* behavior of learning algorithms with theorems and mathematical proofs and the latter addresses the *specific* behavior of learning algorithms by examining their performance on particular tasks.

It should not be surprising that the field of grammatical inference breaks down this way. In computer science, we want to know our algorithms work as intended. This requires a well-defined problem space and well-defined criteria for solutions for every problem instance. It is helpful to compare the situation to a simpler one. In introductory computer science courses we learn which procedures can sort lists. There are many algorithms that can do this such as (for instance) bubble sort. Importantly, the problem space is well defined. The inputs to the problem contain any finite list of elements in addition to an ordering relation over those elements. The success criteria are also well defined. The job of the algorithm is to return a new list with the elements of the input list sorted according to the ordering relation. It is a theoretical result that bubble sort correctly solves this problem for *any* of the possible inputs.

We can consider a world before bubble sort (or any other sorting algorithm) had been discovered. How could we reliably sort lists in such a world? One method may have been to develop procedures and to test their performance on individual lists. Does the procedure seem to do its job on lists A, B, and C? If so, we may hope that it does well on lists D and E as well. Of course, without a theoretical result, there would be no guarantee the procedure performs well on D and E. On the other hand, efforts to successfully sort lists A, B, and C may well lead to such a theoretical result.

In other words, when trying to address any problem computationally, there are two fronts with which it can be addressed: the formal front and the empirical one. Grammatical inference is a research program working at both these levels. The formal approach is concerned with defining the problem space and proving that an algorithm satisfies the solution criteria for any instance of the problem space. Progress is made when learning problems are identified and algorithms developed which provably solve them. The problems can vary in their instance space and their success criteria. This is why we say formal grammatical inference is concerned with ascertaining the *general* behavior of algorithms which are engaged in learning. Given an initial set of assumptions about the input to the learning algorithm, can we guarantee a certain level of performance?

On the other hand, empirical grammatical inference is more concerned with improving the *specific* behavior of algorithms engaged in learning. These algorithms are usually run for particular tasks for which particular inputs are already present. For instance, given a particular training corpus of data as input, can we improve the output of the algorithm so that it performs better according to some metrics on a particular test set of data? The empirical approach tries to get something to work well for one case, and then another, and then another. This approach is often motivated by deploying quickly a system which works for the immediate cases at hand.

Part of the issue researchers face in the computational science of learning is precisely stating what the instance space and success criteria are. This is one reason why formal grammatical inference is difficult (but also exciting). Where one chooses to work is a matter of personal preference. But there can be little doubt about the ultimate importance of the formal work. One only needs to consider where we would be without theoretical guarantees for sorting algorithms (and many other kinds of algorithms) to see why. This does not lessen the importance of empirical approaches. Not only are they often crucial intermediate stages in developing formal results, they are also more immediately applicable to tasks we wish to automate today. An incomplete solution to a problem is never as good as a complete solution, but it is much better than no solution whatsoever.

The situation in computational linguistics can also be understood in these terms. There are many problems which need to be addressed: transliteration, machine translation, anaphora resolution, etc. On the one hand, we want to define a problem, understand its instance space and solutions, and prove that a particular algorithm solves this problem, preferably efficiently. This is formal grammatical inference. On the other hand, however, in the absence of such results that can be immediately deployed for everyday useful tasks, empirical grammatical inference develops learning systems that aim to be immediately useful on particular tasks or particular problem instances.

There are many other ways to look at the learning of (natural language) grammars. For instance, one area of research aims to develop cognitive models of language learning. In this area, properties of theoretical models are compared against the performance of human learners. It still is not clear exactly what a cognitively realistic model of language learning should include. Another approach has been called evolutionary language learning. It models language learning over generations. Once the learner has learned a model, it becomes the oracle of the next generation. These models are often investigated as social processes, with multiple oracles and multiple learners. These kinds of views on learning are beyond the scope of this book.

The next two sections provide an introduction in the two areas discussed in this book. First, formal grammatical inference will be introduced, followed by empirical grammatical inference. The rest of the book follows a similar line. In Chapter 2, formal grammatical inference is discussed in detail. Chapter 3 concentrates on learning *regular* languages (see below), primarily from the perspective of formal grammatical inference, although some empirical grammatical inference algorithms are mentioned. Chapter 4 deals with learning non-regular languages, and mostly in the context of empirical grammatical inference (though again some formal grammatical inference algorithms are mentioned). Finally, Chapter 5 summarizes the field, describes open questions, and highlights lessons learned so far.

1.3   FORMAL GRAMMATICAL INFERENCE

During the informal description of grammatical inference in the first part of this chapter, we already mentioned some possible choices for modeling the learning process. In order to allow us to be explicit about what the entire process looks like, we will have to come up with a way of describing all the details of the process. Essentially, the same holds for the descriptive power of our grammar (which is going to describe the language that we are aiming to learn). Fortunately, the language of mathematics allows us to formally describe the learning process as well as the model of the language.

Having mathematical descriptions of the grammar and the learning process allows us to reason about the possibilities (and impossibilities) of (efficient) learnability. In other words, we can mathematically prove whether it is possible that a particular language (or group of languages) is learnable in that particular learning setting.

Before we can come up with mathematical proofs, we need to formalize all aspects of the learning process. When modeling language learning in a mathematical way, we need to have formal descriptions of the language we are trying to learn and a representation (a grammar) that allows us to represent the language we are learning. Additionally, we will need to describe the learning process, which consists of a description of how the interaction between the oracle, which provides information on the language, and the learner takes place as well as how success of learning is measured. Together, all of these items will determine the instance space of the learning problem.

In the next three sections, we will describe each of the aspects in more detail. First, we will take a look at the relationship between languages and their representation. Second, we describe how languages can be grouped in families according to linguistic properties the languages share. Finally, we will focus on properties of the learning process and indicate that the learnability proofs can be based on properties of language families, which allows us to generalize learnability from one language to a family of languages.

1.3.1   LANGUAGE AND GRAMMAR

From a formal perspective, a language is seen as a set of strings. This set may be finite or infinite and the corresponding language is called finite or infinite, respectively. For instance, the language that describes all English words representing the numbers from 1 to 10 is finite: {one, two, three, four, five, six, seven, eight, nine, ten}. Obviously, finite languages may still be very large; for instance, imagine the formal language containing all possible English sentences with fewer than 100 words.[1] This language is finite, but quite large.

Representing a finite language can be done by simply enumerating all strings in the set. The case of infinite languages is harder, because we would like to represent the infinite language with finite means (time, amount of paper, etc.). In order to represent an infinite set with finite means, we need an additional syntax to describe the exact way in which the infinite set is represented.

Imagine we want to describe the language that contains of all strings that consist of any number of a's: {a, aa, aaa, . . . }. In the previous sentence, we have already provided two informal "grammars" which describe the right language in finite ways. The first used a natural language description: "the language that contains all strings that consist of any number of a's". This description, which contains 13 words, is a finite description of this language. The second relied on some syntax, namely the

---

1. Technically, one would require a finite alphabet, so only words "from the dictionary" are allowed.

symbols: . . . , {, and }. Additionally, we have used a comma and a list of example strings. If we give a description of the language using these symbols, we presume that the reader of the informal grammar understands what we mean by these symbols. In this informal way, we can communicate which infinite language we are thinking of with a finite means using the words and notation above.

Describing a language using a grammar requires a notation and an interpretation of this notation. In the previous paragraph we have used an informal (natural language) and somewhat less informal description with some mathematical symbols. Informal descriptions have several disadvantages. First, they are often ambiguous. In our natural language description, for instance, it is unclear whether the empty string—the string which has no as or any other symbols—is also part of the language or not. Second, there are many different ways to describe the same language. Some descriptions may be quite understandable, but for others it may be very hard to figure out exactly what language they represent. Third, informal descriptions can make it hard to identify important properties of the language.

Using formal descriptions of languages solves most of the problems of informal descriptions. In the case of formal descriptions, the language is described using symbols that have a predefined meaning. First, formal descriptions are unambiguous. The "grammar" of mathematics describes exactly how we should combine symbols into a coherent, meaningful whole. Additionally, each symbol has its own meaning or interpretation that we all agree on. Note that this requires that we all need to agree on how these symbols are used. This is why Section 1.6 contains an overview of the mathematical notations used in this book.[2]

To summarize, we want to be able to describe languages, which may be infinite. To represent the languages, we require grammars. Each grammar (which is guaranteed to be finite) represents its own (possibly infinite) language through an interpretation. To describe the language in a finite, unambiguous way, a grammar is denoted using mathematical symbols.

Having access to mathematical descriptions of formal languages clearly has advantages, as discussed above. However, if our aim is to say something about learning natural languages, we need to know which kinds of grammars can describe the aspects of natural languages that we are interested in.

Currently, there is still some debate about which formalism will allow us to describe natural languages most accurately. A range of formalisms is being used to describe natural languages. For instance, several context-sensitive formalisms are currently being investigated for their ability to naturally and efficiently describe aspects of natural language syntax, such as multiple context-free grammars (MCFGs), minimalist grammars (MGs), and Tree-Adjoining Grammars (TAGs)

---

2. We realize that this reasoning does not completely hold, because we describe the mathematical symbols using (potentially ambiguous) natural language. However, the problem of ambiguity is reduced by describing the meaning of the symbols as much as possible out of context. This means that the meaning is described in a generic way.

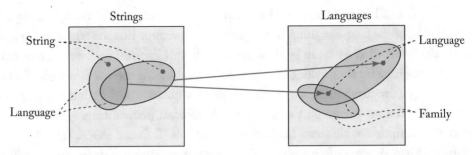

FIGURE 1.2: The relationship between strings, languages, and language families.

[Joshi 1985, Seki et al. 1991, Stabler 1997, 2011]. Also in wide use in natural language processing are finite-state acceptors and transducers, which are different (but related) kinds of finite-state grammars. Grammar formalisms such as these will be defined as they are needed throughout the book.

1.3.2   LANGUAGE FAMILIES

So far, we have talked about ways of describing a specific language. It is tempting to think of a specific, particular language as the target of the learning problem. However, this is a mistake akin to thinking of the sorting problem as the problem of sorting a *specific* list. A particular language is an *instance* of a more general problem, just like a particular list is an *instance* of the more general sorting problem.

A collection of languages is called a *family* of languages. For instance, a language that only contains a finite number of strings is called a *finite* language. The family of finite languages is the set containing all and only such languages. In a similar line, natural languages are all and only those languages spoken or written by people. More generally, a family of languages can be defined in terms of one or more *properties*.

Figure 1.2 visualizes the relationship between strings, languages and families of languages. The left square describes the collection of all possible strings. A dot in that square represents a specific string. This square should be understood to contain all logically possibly strings (and thus infinitely many strings). A language, represented by an ellipse in the figure, describes a (possibly infinite) set of strings belonging to the language. The right square represents the collection of all possible *languages*. A dot in the right square represents one language. One such language corresponds to an ellipse in the left square. An ellipse in the right square denotes a family of languages, which is a (possibly infinite) set of languages.

One issue which arises when defining a learning problem is defining the set of learning targets. One way this has been accomplished is with language families. For example, for *any* language L in

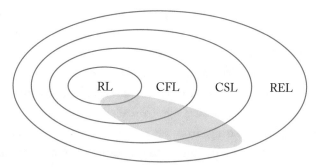

FIGURE 1.3: The Chomsky Hierarchy, with REL: recursively enumerable languages; CSL: context-sensitive languages; CFL: context-free languages; and RL: regular languages. The semitransparent ellipse represents a cross-cutting class.

this family, it would be desirable at the end of the learning process that the learning algorithm outputs a grammar which is an accurate description of L. With regard to natural languages, it would be desirable to find a class of formal languages which is sufficiently expressive to describe some aspect of natural languages, and to make this the set of learning targets.

It is useful to mention at this point that formal language theory has investigated many families of languages, and has achieved remarkable success in understanding how these families are related and the different grammatical formalisms that can be used to generate, represent, and distinguish languages in these families. The Chomsky Hierarchy includes the most well-known languages in this class and is shown in Figure 1.3. The languages in each family are united by their common property of being expressible with a particular grammatical formalism. Section 1.6 provides formal definitions for these grammars and families of languages.

There are several other, less well-known, families of languages that have been studied and new families of languages are being identified. These families cross-cut the families in the Chomsky Hierarchy and include both subregular classes and non-regular classes. While formal grammatical inference clearly addresses learning problems where the families of the Chomsky Hierarchy make up the learning targets, it is also interested in other families of languages as well.

1.3.3   LEARNING LANGUAGES EFFICIENTLY

Thus, one aim of formal grammatical inference can be said to identify families of languages and develop algorithms that provably efficiently learn languages within the family in a particular learning setting. With respect to computational linguistics, the aim can be said to find a formal description of a family of languages that can be said to contain all natural languages, and at the same time can be shown to be efficiently learnable in a learning setting that corresponds most closely to the real world (for instance, the learning setting that most closely corresponds to human early life).

Describing a learning setting requires two design choices. First, what does the process of interaction between the learner and the oracle look like? In one setting, it might be the case that the oracle simply provides information, which the learner can use. The information may only include examples of valid strings from a target language (so-called positive data) or it may only include examples of both valid and invalid strings from the target language (positive and negative data). In another setting, the learner might be permitted to question the oracle regarding whether strings belong to the target language and the oracle may be required to answer truthfully. Questions on how to deal with oracles which are sometimes untruthful (i.e., noise), and implicit or explicit feedback of the oracle also belong to this design choice.

The second design choice regards what constitutes a successful solution to the learning problem. One setting might require the grammar output by the learner to represent a language which is identical to the language of the oracle. Alternatively, the learning setting may allow the grammar to represent a language which differs from the language of the oracle, but the errors are limited in some way. Settings can also be used to impose efficiency conditions on learning algorithms which limit the number of computations it can make during the process. Consequently, an algorithm which is successful at learning a family of languages in a setting with no efficiency conditions may fail to learn the same family in a setting which imposes some. The choice of setting defines what "learning" means.

Results in formal grammatical inference are proofs of theorems whose statements are something like "Algorithm A in learning setting S successfully learns the family of languages $\mathcal{L}$". The setting S contains all the important details about the kind of information the learner receives, the requests it makes, and what counts as success. We find it interesting that the proofs of these theorems often rely on a subtle interplay between the requirements of the learning setting S and the *properties* of the family of languages $\mathcal{L}$. Different learning settings, families of language, and learnability results are described in Chapters 2 and 3.

1.4   EMPIRICAL GRAMMATICAL INFERENCE

Empirical grammatical inference starts with the notion that natural languages are efficiently learnable because people manage to learn them. This means that the language should be learnable given an appropriate input. If we can develop systems that are able to learn these languages, we can then analyze properties of these systems. The identified properties can form the basis of learnability proofs in the area of formal grammatical inference. At the same time, empirical grammatical inference leads to deployable systems that work well enough to be used in tasks involving the learning of natural languages.

Empirical grammatical inference is also motivated in part by the following concerns. First, for most, if not all, natural languages, we do not have a complete and correct grammatical representation available. For grammatical inference, this means that the model of the oracle (M_O in Figure 1.1) cannot be made explicit in any way. It also means that we do not know exactly where the family of natural languages is located in the hierarchy represented in Figure 1.2.

A second concern is that there is a debate on exactly how the interaction between the oracle (say, the parent) and the learner (the child) occurs. It is clear that the learner receives example strings, such as sentences, or words, from the oracle. For instance, the oracle (parent) speaks to the learner (child). However, the learner may perhaps also receive additional information, in the shape of non-verbal communication, such as the oracle pointing to objects. Additionally, the learner can also speak to the oracle and if the oracle reacts in a certain way, the learner may believe that the oracle correctly interpreted the utterance and this may also be a source of information for the learner.

The combination of language representation with the shape of the interaction leads to additional choices. Perhaps the language representation should be able to encode semantic information. If this is possible, it leads to the additional problem that the semantics also need to be learned and grounded in the real world or the learner's model of the real world.

The same questions that need to be asked in the field of formal grammatical inference to design learning settings (language family, learning process and evaluation) are just as relevant in the field of empirical grammatical inference. However, due to the different starting point of empirical grammatical inference with respect to its formal counterpart, some distinct choices are made. These will be discussed briefly in the following sections and in more detail in Chapters 3 and 4.

1.4.1 LANGUAGES, GRAMMARS, AND LANGUAGE FAMILIES

Like formal grammatical inference, empirical grammatical inference systems learn from example strings, such as sentences or words. Depending on the type of string, different languages are learned, for instance, the language of natural language sentences, which corresponds to describing syntax, or the language of words, which requires a grammar of morphology.

Also, like the algorithms developed in formal grammatical inference, the outputs of empirical grammatical inference algorithms are grammars. However, unlike formal grammatical inference, the target of learning is not necessarily a family of languages. The ultimate aim of an empirical grammatical inference system is to be able to learn the language that underlies the input data it is given. This means that the learning system should essentially be language independent. This does not necessarily mean that the same system should be able to learn every aspect (syntax, morphology, etc.) of every natural language. Some systems may focus on identifying word boundaries in a stream of phonemes, learning rules of word or sentence formation, or something else. The only requirement is that the description of the language is done according to a grammar (which, just like in formal grammatical inference, is a finite representation of the language).

One difference between formal and empirical grammatical inference is that the target of empirical grammatical inference can be construed as one or a small number of particular languages, whereas the target of formal grammatical inference is a class of languages. As we discuss below, empirical grammatical inference uses data from a small number of specific languages, and the performance of the system is measured by comparing the learned grammar against a gold standard, which is taken to be their grammars, which are known only to an oracle.

1.4.2   EVALUATION

The evaluation methods discussed in the context of formal grammatical inference measures the performance of learning algorithms *in vitro* (or perhaps better named *in silico*). In this situation, the problem space is known in advance and so are the solutions to the problem instances. What is unknown is an algorithm which maps problem instances to their solutions. However, once an algorithm is proposed, evaluation can proceed in part by comparing its output on a problem instance directly against (a grammar of) the target language. In contrast, research in the area of empirical grammatical inference measures the performance of empirical systems *in vivo*. The performance of the systems is measured in the context of an application. Thus, empirical grammatical inference systems can be evaluated both *extrinsically* by using the algorithm as a component in a larger system and *intrinsically* by comparing measures like precision and recall to a gold standard.

The aim of empirical grammatical inference systems is to learn the grammar of the language which performs best on some task, or range of tasks, as possible. Thus, in empirical grammatical inference, the problem is one of optimization: What algorithm exists that outputs a grammar whose behavior on a task is optimal?

Obviously then, to know exactly *how* well the learned grammar behaves, evaluation criteria are needed. Different situations may require different evaluation criteria to determine how well the system is doing. For instance, if we are interested in learning only specific syntactic constructions, there is no need to evaluate against the entire target language. We only want to know to what extent the constructions we are interested in are being learned correctly.

Ideally, for the problem of language identification, the learned grammar (that of the learner, M_L) should completely cover the target language (described by M_O) while at the same time no additional strings (not part of the target language) should be accepted by the learned grammar. Even though the system should learn the language completely and correctly, in practical situations (for example in which no full description of the target grammar is known, such as in the case of natural languages) this proves to be difficult. Evaluation metrics that indicate to what extent the grammar is complete and correct show us how close we are to a particular goal.

Another way empirical grammatical inference algorithms can be evaluated is via their incorporation into pre-existing natural language processing systems. Applications that deal with strings, such as speech-driven dialog systems and information extraction systems, often need to know how to deal with unexpected input. In the case of natural languages, this may, for instance, be in the form of new words or syntactic constructions. Since grammatical inference algorithms generalize beyond their input, incorporating a learning algorithm in an application may be used to make the application more robust in dealing with unexpected input. If incorporating the grammatical inference system (or an alternative implementation of such a system) improves the performance of the overall application, then we can attribute the increase in performance to the newly added grammatical inference module.

1.5 SUMMARY

To summarize, both formal and empirical grammatical inference have their roles to play in computational linguistics. While the two areas of research may seem quite different, there are quite a few similarities.

At the start of both research processes, one of the first questions one encounters is the *bias decision* (see Section 2.5 for a discussion on bias), which consists of making a guess about which grammars correspond best with the language(s) we are trying to learn. Exactly which class of grammars is selected is based on at least two reasons. First, we need to believe that the class of grammars we select is going to be strong enough to be able to describe the language(s) we are trying to learn and that it has other properties, such as probabilistic variants, necessary for the problem at hand. Second, algorithms which can learn these grammars from some input should either be inadequate in some way or non-existent. Otherwise, it would not be research!

Both formal and empirical grammatical inference are attempting to learn grammars from data (either explicitly present or not). The techniques used can be very similar, if not identical. The primary difference is how success is measured. In formal learning, we are primarily going to measure success by transforming an ill-posed learning problem into a (mathematically) well-posed one and proving an algorithm solves this problem. For the result to be useful in a deployable system, it must be the case that the problem we face in the real world is an instance of this formal problem. If not, then all bets are off. For example, an algorithm which provably efficiently learns a family of languages probably will not be very effective in a natural language processing system if natural languages do not belong to this family of formal languages.

In empirical learning we will (usually) be measuring success with respect to a gold standard, which is a proxy for the "true" answer. This type of evaluation does not make the assumption that what we had to learn belongs to one family or another: the aim is to learn a grammar whose behavior on some task is as close as possible to the gold standard (according to the evaluation metric).

1.6   FORMAL PRELIMINARIES

In order to be precise when discussing learning, it is essential that the meaning of all the terminology is clear. In this section we will introduce several concepts that will be used throughout the book.

However, we will assume the readers are familiar with certain concepts and notation. For instance, we assume a basic familiarity with *set theory* and its notation, such as the empty set ($\varnothing$), union, intersection, and set difference ($\cup, \cap, \setminus$). Moreover, given a set X, we will write $|X|$ for the cardinality of X. The symmetric difference between two sets (or languages) A and B is $A \oplus B = (A \setminus B) \cup (B \setminus A)$.

We also assume familiarity with the *standard logic* and will make use of the logical connectives representing "and," "or," negation, implication, and bi-conditional ($\wedge, \vee, \neg, \Rightarrow, \Leftrightarrow$, respectively), the universal and existential quantifiers ($\forall, \exists$, respectively).

We also assume a basic familiarity with *computational complexity theory* and an understanding of $\mathcal{O}$ notation and awareness of terms such as $\mathcal{P}, \mathcal{NP}$, and $\mathcal{NP}$-complete. For readers unfamiliar with these terms, we recommend the following texts: Garey and Johnson [1979] and Cormen [2013].

Grammatical inference deals with learning representations of languages. This requires us to be precise about what a language is. Informally, a language contains strings. These strings are made up out of symbols. These symbols come from the vocabulary.

Definition 1.1 (Vocabulary or alphabet)   A *vocabulary* or *alphabet* is a finite, non-empty set of symbols Σ.

In the natural language context, for instance, a vocabulary might be the set of words, when describing syntax (with the potential problem that it is possible to generate new words, for instance through compounding, which might lead to a theoretically infinite set of symbols), or phonemes, when describing phonological representations.

Based on the vocabulary, we can create strings, which may also be called sequences.

Definition 1.2 (String)   A (finite) string $w = a_1 \ldots a_n$ is a possibly empty, finite, ordered list of symbols. We write λ for the unique string of length 0 (called the empty string) and $|w|$ for the length of w. Thus $n = |w|$. Σ^* denotes the set of all finite strings over Σ.

With strings we can now define languages.

Definition 1.3 (Language)   A language L is a possibly infinite set of strings: $L \subseteq \Sigma^\star$. Let $\mathbb{N}$ denote the set of non-negative integers. For all $k \in \mathbb{N}$, let $\Sigma^{\leq k} = \{w \in \Sigma^\star : |w| \leq k\}$ and $\Sigma^{>k} = \{w \in \Sigma^\star : |w| > k\}$.

We say that u is a *subsequence* of v, denoted $u \preceq v$, if_{def} $u = a_1 \ldots a_{|u|}$ and there exist $v_0, \ldots, v_{|u|} \in \Sigma^\star$ s.t. $v = v_0 a_1 v_1 \ldots a_{|u|} v_{|u|}$.

We say that u is a *substring* of v if_{def} there exist two strings l and r, possibly empty, such that $v = lur$.

For any finite set of strings L, we let $\|L\|$ be the sum of the lengths of the strings in L. We will write $|L|$ for the cardinality of L.

The *concatenation* of two languages L_1 and L_2 is written $L_1 L_2$ and is defined to be $L_1 L_2 = \{wv \mid w \in L_1 \text{ and } v \in L_2\}$. It is also useful to define the Kleene star operation with respect to languages. The Kleene star of a language L is another language written L^* and is defined recursively: $\lambda \in L^*$ and for all $w \in L$, $w \in L^*$ (the base cases) and $w, v \in L^* \Rightarrow wv \in L^*$ (the recursive case).

Note that the formal descriptions of languages, symbols in Σ and strings from $\Sigma^\star$ are simply formal concepts. Depending on what symbols are available in Σ and hence can be used in $\Sigma^\star$, people might assign specific meaning to these symbols, strings, and languages. However, from a formal perspective, these definitions do not require the assignment of a particular meaning. To describe exactly which strings are an element of a particular language, a representation of the language is required. This is done using a grammar.

Definition 1.4 (Grammar)   A *grammar* G_L is a finite representation that describes a (possibly infinite) language L.

Exactly how a grammar describes the infinite language depends on how it is interpreted. While a grammar defines just one language, languages which admit common grammar formalisms (i.e., a common notation and interpretation) form a family of languages.[3] It is useful in this regard to define classes of grammars and the families of languages that are associated with them.

Definition 1.5 (Language and grammar families)   A class of languages $\mathcal{L}$ is represented by the grammars of a class $\mathcal{G}$. $\mathcal{L}$ and $\mathcal{G}$ are related by a naming function $\mathbb{L} : \mathcal{G} \to \mathcal{L}$ that is total ($\forall G \in \mathcal{G}, \mathbb{L}(G) \in \mathcal{L}$) and surjective ($\forall L \in \mathcal{L}, \exists G \in \mathcal{G}$ such that $\mathbb{L}(G) = L$).

In words, any language in $\mathcal{L}$ admits a grammar from $\mathcal{G}$. For any string $w \in \Sigma^\star$ and language $L \in \mathcal{L}$, we will write $L \models w$ if_{def} $w \in L$. This corresponds to the notion of being able to recognize

---

3. Technically, there is a difference between a *family* (the family of regular languages), which is an abstract notion but not a set, and a *class* of languages over some fixed alphabet Σ. In the latter case, mathematical manipulations are possible. We will nevertheless not make this difference in the sequel, and use freely both terms, with an implicit alphabet when so required.

whether string w belongs to language L. Additionally, the grammars should be understood as allowing a given *parser* (whatever it may look like) to recognize the strings. For any string $w \in \Sigma^{\star}$ and grammar $G \in \mathcal{G}$, we will write $G \vdash w$ if the parser recognizes w. Basically, the parser must be sound and complete with respect to the interpretation: $G \vdash w \iff \mathbb{L}(G) \models w$.

There are many ways to write grammars. Mathematically, grammars can be sets of strings, or tuples of sets or other finite objects. It is possible to develop universal coding systems; for example, sets and tuples themselves can be expressed as finite strings (in fact, every finite string, and thus grammar) can be expressed with a unique positive integer [Rogers 1967]). Thus, the naming function and the finite grammar itself are deeply interwoven concepts. Together, they allow us to decide what strings are recognized by the (potentially infinite) language the grammar describes. Consequently, there are several ways languages can be described. We illustrate this diversity of grammars with the regular languages.

One particular grammar formalism is that of deterministic finite-state acceptors.

Definition 1.6 (Deterministic finite-state acceptor (DFA))   A *deterministic finite-state acceptor* is a quintuple $\langle \Sigma, Q, q_0, F, \delta \rangle$ for which

- Σ is the finite set of input symbols, corresponding to the vocabulary;

- $Q = \{q_0, q_1, \ldots, q_{N-1}\}$ is the finite set of N states;

- q_0 is the start state;

- F is the finite set of final states ($F \subseteq Q$); and

- $\delta : Q \times \Sigma \to Q$ is the transition function. Given a state $q \in Q$ and input symbol $i \in \Sigma$, either $\delta(q, i)$ is undefined or it returns a state $q' \in Q$.

We refer to the class of DFA with $\mathcal{G}_{DFA}$. We also let the size of a DFA be given by its number of states: $\|\langle \Sigma, Q, q_0, F, \delta \rangle\| \equiv |Q|$.

How do we identify the strings recognized by a DFA? In other words, what is the naming function? How are these objects interpreted? These questions are answered as follows. For each DFA, δ recursively defines a function $\delta^* : Q \times \Sigma^{\star} \to Q$. For all $q \in Q$, let $\delta^*(q, \lambda) = q$ and, for all $u \in \Sigma^{\star}, a \in \Sigma$, let $\delta^*(q, ua) = \delta(\delta^*(q, u), a)$. (If $\delta^*(q, u)$ is undefined or if for some $q \in Q$ and $a \in \Sigma$, $\delta(q, a)$ is undefined then $\delta^*(q, ua)$ would then also be undefined). For each DFA A, the language of A is $\mathbb{L}(A) = \{w \in \Sigma^{\star} \mid \delta^*(q_0, w) \in F\}$. The class of *regular* languages contain exactly those languages for which a DFA exists which describes it.

Definition 1.7 (Family of regular languages) $\mathcal{L}_{RL} = \{L \mid (\exists A \in \mathcal{G}_{DFA})[\mathbb{L}(A) = L]\}$

Note that other representations, such as regular expressions (also used in several programming languages), can also be used to describe exactly all regular languages.

Definition 1.8 (Regular expression)   Given Σ, a *regular expression* is defined recursively as follows.

1. The *base cases:*

    1. $\varnothing$ is a regular expression.

    2. λ is a regular expression.

    3. For all $\sigma \in \Sigma$, σ is a regular expression.

2. The *recursive cases:*

    1. If R is a regular expression then (R^*) is a regular expression.

    2. If R and S are regular expressions then (RS) is a regular expression.

    3. If R and S are regular expressions then $(R + S)$ is a regular expression.

3. Nothing else is a regular expression.

While the definition above is suggestive, it is important to realize regular expressions are just strings of uninterpretable symbols at this stage. To relate them to languages, we will need to make use of an explicit naming function. This is accomplished recursively as follows.

1. The *base cases:*

    1. $\mathbb{L}(\varnothing) = \varnothing$

    2. $\mathbb{L}(\lambda) = \{\lambda\}$

    3. $\forall \sigma \in \Sigma, \mathbb{L}(\sigma) = \{\sigma\}$

2. The *recursive cases:*

    1. $\mathbb{L}(R^*) = (\mathbb{L}(R))^*$

    2. $\mathbb{L}(RS) = \mathbb{L}(R)\mathbb{L}(S)$

    3. $\mathbb{L}(R + S) = \mathbb{L}(R) \cup \mathbb{L}(S)$

    The following theorem is a remarkable fact.

Theorem 1.1 (Kleene's Theorem)   Every language definable with a regular expression is definable with a DFA and vice versa.

    Another grammar formalism is that of context-free grammars (CFGs).

Definition 1.9 (Context-free grammar)   A *context-free grammar* is a quadruple $G = \langle V, \Sigma, S, R \rangle$ for which

- V, the finite set of non-terminals;

- Σ, the finite set of terminals;

- $S \in V$, the start non-terminal; and

- $R \subset V \times (V \cup \Sigma)^*$ is the set of productions (grammar rules).

For all $(A, \beta) \in R$, we often write $A \to \beta$. We refer to the class of CFGs with $\mathcal{G}_{CFG}$.

Again, we can ask what is the naming function for context-free grammars? How are they interpreted? The language of a context-free grammar is defined as follows. The (partial) *derivations* of a CFG $G = \langle V, \Sigma, S, R \rangle$ is written $D(G)$ and is defined recursively as follows.

1. The *base case:* S belongs to $D(G)$.

2. The *recursive case:* For all $A \rightarrow \beta \in R$ and for all $\gamma_1, \gamma_2 \in (V \cup \Sigma)^*$, if $\gamma_1 A \gamma_2 \in D(G)$ then $\gamma_1 \beta \gamma_2 \in D(G)$.

3. Nothing else is in $D(G)$.

Then the language of the grammar $\mathbb{L}(G)$ is defined as $\mathbb{L}(G) = \{w \in \Sigma^\star \mid w \in D(G)\}$.

Based on the definition of context-free grammars, we can define context-free languages.

Definition 1.10 (Family of context-free languages) $\mathcal{L}_{CF} = \{L \mid (\exists G \in \mathcal{G}_{CFG})[\mathbb{L}(G) = L]\}$

It is another remarkable fact that every regular language is context-free, but not vice versa.

Theorem 1.2 ([Scott and Rabin 1959])   Regular languages are a proper subset of context-free languages.

The two theorems above show what is possible when a grammar formalism is introduced. They help realize what the expressive power of the grammar formalism is.

The Chomsky Hierarchy (Figure 1.3) describes the expressive power between four well-known families of languages: regular languages (also called type 3), context-free languages (type 2), context-sensitive languages (type 1), and recursively enumerable languages (type 0). The first two have already been defined.

Context-sensitive languages can be described using context-sensitive grammars, which are very similar to context-free grammars, with the difference that all productions in R are of the form $\alpha A \beta \rightarrow \alpha \gamma \beta$ with $A \in V$, α and $\beta \in (V \cup \Sigma)^*$, and $\gamma \in (V \cup \Sigma)^+$. Recursively enumerable languages (also called computably enumerable) are languages for which a Turing machine exists that, for every string in the language, correctly answers "yes" if asked whether the string belongs to the language.[4]

If context-free languages are more powerful than regular languages, why even consider or use regular languages? Or, in that same line of reasoning, why even consider context-free languages and not go all the way for recursively enumerable languages?

---

4. The Turing machine can be thought of as a grammar for this language. Note it does not have to answer if asked about a string which does *not* belong to the language. Languages for which there exists a Turing machine which has to answer correctly about the membership of every string in $\Sigma^\star$ form the recursive class of languages. This class is a proper subset of the recursively enumerable languages and properly contains the context-sensitive languages.

One answer is that there appears to be a trade-off between generative power and efficiency. For instance, recognizing membership of strings in regular languages can be done in linear time, $T(n) = \mathcal{O}(n)$; recognizing membership in context-free languages can be done in cubic time, $T(n) = \mathcal{O}(n^3)$; and for more powerful language families, such as context-sensitive languages, this is worse. In fact, it is $\mathcal{P}$-space complete.[5]

Another reason comes from the perspective that scientific theories and hypotheses ought to be strong and falsifiable. So if one's theory of natural language is that anything computable is a natural language then that is the weakest theory possible that makes no falsifiable predictions (at least under the Church–Turing thesis). It follows that the hypothesis that all natural languages are describable with DFAs is a stronger scientific hypothesis than the one that says all natural languages are describable with CFGs. The evidence is, however, that this hypothesis is not correct [Chomsky 1956, Shieber 1985].

It is for these reasons that the goal to identify the smallest family of languages that contains all possible human languages (or the smallest family of languages relevant to some aspect of human language) is reasonable. This may not necessarily be one of the families in the Chomsky Hierarchy; instead it may be one that cross-cuts those classes as shown in Figure 1.3.

---

5. In complexity theory, a problem is said to be $\mathcal{P}$-space complete if it is *hardest* between all problems which can be solved with a Turing machine which uses memory polynomial in the size of its input. The generally accepted conjecture is that this means that no reasonable (polynomial-time) algorithm exists.

CHAPTER 2

Formal Learning

2.1 INTRODUCTION

The goal of this chapter is to show a global picture of the formal issues and results in grammatical inference. A more extensive survey can be found in de la Higuera [2010]. The theory underlying grammatical inference rests upon a number of pillars such as the theory of languages and automata [Sudkamp 2006], their probabilistic counterparts such as hidden Markov models [Rabiner 1989], and basic concepts from computational complexity [Sanjeev and Boaz 2009], computational learning theory [Kearns and Vazirani 1994], and information theory [Cover and Thomas 1991].

2.1.1 THE ISSUES OF LEARNING

Grammatical inference is about learning a *grammar* given information about a *language*. Generally speaking, the information a *learner* is going to have access to concerns a language: if in linguistic terms a language may have a meaning rendered complex by the point of view with which one is approaching these questions, in mathematics a language is just a set of strings.[1] This set may be infinite, each string having some simple semantic feature associated with it, which may be just a label indicating if the string belongs to the language or not, or, more informatively, the structure (or parse tree) of the string, or even its probability depending on some given distribution. The learner might be given access to a large quantity of sentences (a corpus), which may be organized, and which may be annotated. The learner is in some settings able to interrogate an expert (or alternative sources of data) in order to obtain responses to queries: Does this string or sentence belong to the language? How can we complete this sentence? What are the most frequent sentences in the language? Can this sentence be annotated? Translated?

With this information the learner's goal is to build a *representation* of the language: the representation will typically be a finite-state machine (which allows one to *recognize* the sentences from the language), a grammar (which can be used to *generate* sentences from the language), or another formalism (a regular expression will *define* the set of sentences in the language).

---

1. As described in the previous chapter.

The fact that a learner will build its own formalism of the intended language poses an interesting question: If two learners build two different-looking grammars, how can they agree that they are using the same language? The answer to this question is in many cases negative: they cannot (the problem of *deciding* equivalence between two grammars, for many classes, is intractable). This is a serious hint that learning grammars is a difficult task. A puzzling scenario allowing us to *solve* the equivalence problem for two grammars G_1 and G_2 could be the following: a learner tries to learn from data generated from G_1, and obtains G'_1, does the same from G_2, obtaining G'_2. Now, should not G'_1 and G'_2 coincide, in a syntactic sense?

When learning only from strings, which is also usually called *unsupervised learning*, an attractive alternative is to build a probabilistic artifact. A probabilistic context-free grammar, a probabilistic finite automaton, or a hidden Markov model will each associate a quantity with a string, typically defining the probability of that string. In this case, the notion of *associated language* may not be meaningful: if we just talk about the language of all strings that have non-null probability then we may have two very different distributions that would be equivalent as far as their associated languages are concerned. Furthermore, this would not even prove useful. Another definition would be to say that a string is in the language when its probability is above a given threshold. This tempting definition leads to severe computational problems as, even in the case where the distribution is produced by a finite-state machine, a number of associated problems are intractable, like (1) knowing if such a language is finite or (2) finding the most probable string.

Probabilistic finite-state automata (PFA) can be seen as a special case of *transducers*: these are finite-state machines taking strings as inputs and also as outputs. In the case of PFA the outputs are probabilities. Generalizing, the output can be a multiplicity or even another string (the translation of the first one). In a broad sense, when grammatical inference deals with transducers, the goal is to learn functions which take as inputs strings.

2.1.2   LEARNING SCENARIOS

Depending on the intended application, the learner will have access to the data in one way or another. The way we receive the data, the price we have to pay for it, or the richness of the information received are all going to matter. Let us explore some typical learning settings.

Batch learning is a situation where we are given a (usually large) number of strings. These strings may come with extra information: a label for each string in the case of a classification task, tags attached to substrings, brackets inside the string, or a weight. Two typical settings are those of *learning from text* where only strings from the language are given to the learner, and *learning from an informant* where the strings from which one is to learn are labeled with 1 or

0 depending on the fact that they belong or not to the language. The learner is supposed to build a hypothesis from this sample.

Online learning is a very typical setting from a theoretical point of view: a learning situation where the learner receives the items of data one after the other and is supposed to build a new hypothesis after having seen each new learning example. Gold [1967] introduced this setting in order to show that certain learning algorithms had strong convergence properties (*identification in the limit*): the infinite process (new example → new hypothesis) is supposed to converge to just one grammar being produced after a finite number of steps, provided some completeness conditions are met concerning the presentation of the examples. It has also been argued that this learning situation is well suited to represent the language acquisition task a child has to face.

Active learning is a setting where no data is available at first, or where only unlabeled data is available. The learner then has not only to learn (generalize, induce, etc.) but to query the environment in order to obtain its data or a labeling of this data. Typically the learner will attempt to find out if a particular string belongs to the language or not (*membership query*) or will ask for some extra information about a string present in the data set.

Interactive learning is a special case close to the previous one—the learner classically attempts to automatically build the model, but will interact with an oracle, through some query system: typically the oracle can intervene by correcting some decision made by the learner.

2.1.3   LEARNING GRAMMARS OF LANGUAGES

A first non-trivial question is that of deciding if we are to learn grammars or languages. If common knowledge tells us that this is about language, about learning or acquiring a language, we will argue that since the goal is to study effective ways of learning, there is always a representation issue. Furthermore, a number of results show that for a given class of languages, there will be considerable differences between learning one type of representation rather than another.

Having decided that we need to learn a grammar, we now have to choose what type of grammar we require. We will discuss in Section 2.3 the different arguments that should be considered when making this choice. For the moment, and without entering into precise definitions which can be found in a number of textbooks and research articles, let us list some of the most common and important types of finite-state machines and grammars:

- finite-state machines that recognize languages: deterministic finite-state automata and their non-deterministic counterparts;

- finite-state machines that define distributions over strings: probabilistic automata or hidden Markov models;

- finite-state machines that describe or generate transductions, or translations from one language to another; and

- context-free grammars that are also used to recognize, generate, and describe more complex structural rules.

2.2   LEARNABILITY: DEFINITIONS AND PARADIGMS

Learning is a complex phenomenon. It has been argued that it is about compression, encoding, discovery of patterns, and even the capacity of forgetting. Let us explore some mathematical definitions in which the convergence of learning, speed, and quantity of resources needed to learn can be analyzed.

2.2.1   BLAME THE DATA, NOT THE ALGORITHM

At first, learning seems to be an ill-posed problem. Suppose we have a learning algorithm which on some data returns a grammar. Why should one learned grammar be better than another? Why should this grammar even be the right grammar? After all, the learner has only had access to a finite quantity of data!

In order to transform the seemingly ill-posed learning question into a well-posed question whose solution does give us insights to what learning can mean, we transform it into a convergence problem. Learning is going to be measured as the convergence toward a stable and good solution. In an ideal world, one would hope to have this convergence depend on a magic number: as soon as a given quantity of information or data is available, the intended grammar would be learned. But many things can go wrong: the data may not be representative or, even when it is, we may be facing some intractable problem. It is therefore necessary to impose some conditions on the data in order to secure a learning result, which will therefore always be read as: provided the data available has a minimal quality (with respect to a target and the criterion we impose), we can ensure that the solution is good. *Ensuring* might still depend on some probabilistic notion, and *good* will often also be probabilistically founded.

2.2.2   A NON-PROBABILISTIC SETTING: IDENTIFICATION IN THE LIMIT

The first important definition is due to Gold [1967]: *identification in the limit*. In this learning setting, the learner has access to a never-ending supply of information about the language to be learned. This may be the actual strings from the language, or labeled strings indicating if they belong or not, or any specifics about the language. The important thing is that the presentation of this information has to be complete: all the possible information has to be presented eventually. For example, if learning from *text*, which is the modality of learning from positive examples only, each string in the language should appear at some point or another.

After receiving each piece of information the learner is to return a hypothesis. For a class of grammars to be *identifiable in the limit* it is required that given any grammar G in the class and any *complete presentation* of $\mathbb{L}(G)$, there is a point where the learner begins to systematically output a hypothesis grammar G' (convergence) and $\mathbb{L}(G') = \mathbb{L}(G)$ (correctness). By a *complete* presentation we mean that each admissible information is presented at least once.

Example 2.1   Let us consider the case of the regular languages. These can be represented with deterministic finite automata (DFA). If the type of information we are learning from consists of examples and counter-examples, the setting is called *learning from an informant*. A complete presentation PRES of a language L will present pairs $(w,1)$ and $(w,0)$ such that on one hand $\{w : (w, 1) \in \text{PRES}\} = L$ and $\{w : (w, 0) \in \text{PRES}\} = \Sigma^{\star} \setminus L$. Then an algorithm which systematically searches for the smallest DFA *consistent* with the information seen so far[2] is going to achieve identification in the limit: at some point all the strings of length up to $2n - 1$ (where n is the number of states in the target DFA) will have appeared and theory tells us that any other DFA consistent with the data is larger than the target. Therefore, DFA are identifiable in the limit from an informant.

Main Learning Results

Gold [1967] proved that any recursively enumerable class of languages was identifiable in the limit from an informant. On the other hand, when learning from text (only positive instances are presented) the situation is drastically different: he proved that any class containing all finite languages and at least one infinite language was not identifiable in the limit. The proof is not trivial, but the reader who wishes for himself to try to invent an algorithm should rapidly become convinced of the impossibility of doing so. This, of course, holds for the regular languages, and most well-known classes.

2.2.3   AN ACTIVE LEARNING SETTING

In active learning, the learner is not directly presented with information, but has to ask for it. It does this by *querying* the *oracle*. A number of different queries have been introduced since the introduction of this model by Angluin [1987]: the most important ones are *membership queries*, in which the learner suggests a string to the oracle and receives the status of this string as answer, and (strong) *equivalence*

---

2. Consistency entails that the (smallest) DFA accepts all the positive examples and rejects all the negative ones. The fact that this particular problem cannot be solved by any polynomial-time algorithm is irrelevant here, but the algorithm RPNI discussed in Section 3.7 does solve this problem efficiently.

queries, in which the oracle is presented with a candidate grammar and is to answer "yes" or provide the learner with a counter-example.

The main difference with the online model is that the learner is now in charge of the learning session: it decides the next step, including the fact that there is a next step. Therefore, it must decide at some point to halt. Learning is achieved if it halts with the correct hypothesis (equivalent to the target).

It should be noted that oracles are both abstract mathematical objects and representative of practical learning situations: when the learner can interrogate the environment, query a human expert, or ask the World Wide Web, there may be the chance of using an active learning algorithm.

Main Learning Results

Without further complexity conditions these settings may lead to specific analyses for researchers in inductive inference, but, probably, computational linguists will not find here what they need. Indeed, even DFA cannot be learned from positive data and membership queries alone: for a class to be learnable, the learner must know when to halt, which means that at most one consistent hypothesis is left in the search space.

2.2.4   INTRODUCING COMPLEXITY

In what precedes we have worried about the capacity of our learning algorithm to converge, *some day*. We obviously need something of more practical use. We want to be able to say that learning takes a reasonable amount of time and energy.

Complexity results usually will depend on the size of an instance of the problem. In the case of learning, the instance comprises the data which is given to the learner, but also the target itself, even if the learner never gets to see this target!

What Should We Count?

We first need to know what we are counting. We are in a practical situation where we are given data and are supposed to build a hypothesis. We are concerned not only with the capacity of building something, but also of doing as well as possible with the data we are given. Moreover, there may be a situation where even if we had as much time as we required, we may not have enough data to be able to build a reasonable hypothesis.

Let us explore briefly some of these ideas.

- The size of what we are learning is obviously an issue: if trying to learn a DFA with three states over a two-symbol alphabet—not a very interesting task for computational linguistics—we will certainly need less data than if we are to learn a complex context-free grammar, with hundreds of rules and over an alphabet made of words from some common language. Note also that since simple (formal) languages can be infinite, the actual cardinality of the language is not a useful measure for complexity.

- The size of the information we have been given: The more information we have to process, the longer we will need.[3] This may seem simple, but how should we measure the actual size of a corpus? Is it the number of strings? The number of different strings? Or, the number of symbols that intervene in those strings, i.e., the sum of the lengths of all strings in the sample? A survey of these questions can be found in de la Higuera et al. [2008].

How Should We Count?

In order to be able to talk about the time needed to learn, we have to make a difference between the real learning problem (usually in the batch learning setting—given a sample S, learn a grammar G) and the online problem used in the analysis: we will suppose that the data arrives to the learner one item at the time, and that the learner is required to build a new hypothesis from the data it has had access to so far.

In this theoretical context one can consider counting a number of things.

- The number of errors before learning. In an online setting, the learning algorithm is presented with a new unlabeled piece of data. Its running hypothesis should be able to classify or label this input string. The *implicit prediction error* measure used by Pitt [1989] counts this number. A good learning algorithm is one that will only make a polynomial number of implicit prediction errors before converging.

- The number of *mind changes* is the number of times the learning algorithm has to modify its hypothesis, before learning. Again, it would seem reasonable that this number varies polynomially with the size of the target.

- Another way of measuring concerns the size of a sample sufficient for learning to take place. This *characteristic sample* may be seen as provided by a *teacher*. If small it could mean that the probability that it appears in a random training sample is high. It should be noticed that some types of grammars admit small characteristic samples, whereas others do not [de la Higuera 1997].

These questions were analyzed by Pitt [1989], de la Higuera [1997, 2010], and Eyraud et al. [2015]. Summarizing, it can be shown that in most models even deterministic finite automata are not polynomially learnable. In some cases, this is the "hardest" class one can learn.

---

3. When learning from data streams, a goal is to limit this factor: the learner is not allowed to memorize all the data. For a first example of grammatical inference in this setting, see Balle et al. [2014b].

2.2.5   A PROBABILISTIC VERSION OF IDENTIFICATION IN THE LIMIT

A probabilistic model (or probabilistic language) is a distribution of probabilities over the set of all strings. When learning a probabilistic model two things change: one still does not have control over the presentation, but one can measure bad luck, i.e., the fact that some important information has not yet appeared. On the other hand, what is to be learned has changed, and one is now interested in learning both a structure and the parameters of this structure.

Horning [1969] proposed to learn probabilistic grammars for natural language processing: since then, this line has been followed by a number of researchers. Strong arguments in favor have been proposed by Clark and Lappin [2011].

The notion of identification in the limit can be extended to cope with learning distributions. In this case, instead of being complete, the presentation of the examples is supposed to follow the distribution which is to be learned. The probability that the empirical distribution of examples is indefinitely very different from the theoretical one is 0: we cannot get a skewed distribution forever.

Therefore, a class of probabilistic grammars is identifiable in the limit with probability 1 if there exists a learning algorithm which, given any grammar in the class is guaranteed to build a grammar G' equivalent to G, after having seen a finite number of examples, with probability 1.

Main Learning Results

Identification in the limit with probability 1 has been studied since Angluin [1988a] who first analyzed the problem and suggested an enumerative algorithm. There are two different issues: identifying the structure and identifying the probabilities. A number of results related to the first question can be found in de la Higuera and Oncina [2004] and Stern-Brocot trees are used in order to identify the probabilities in de la Higuera and Thollard [2000].

2.2.6   PROBABLY APPROXIMATELY CORRECT (PAC) LEARNING

The *Probably Approximately Correct* (PAC) paradigm was introduced by Valiant [1984] and has been widely used in machine learning.

In order to define PAC learning, a number of extra parameters have to be introduced:

- n, a parameter measuring the size of the target under scrutiny (typically the number of states, for a finite-state machine);

- m, an upper bound on the length of the strings we want to classify;

- ϵ, the error one is prepared to accept; and

- δ, the confidence with which we want to be within the error.

About Distances

In PAC learning, the goal is to approximate a target grammar G_T by a hypothesis grammar G_H. In order to measure how close G_H is to G_T a distance is required. There are two cases to consider.

- G_T is a (classifying) grammar defining a language, and an independent underlying, but unknown distribution $\mathcal{D}$ exists. This distribution reflects the importance of the data: we expect that a string w_1 whose probability p_1 is double of that of another string w_2 would therefore be twice as frequent in a random sample as w_2. It should be noted that this does not mean that w_1 has probability p_1 of being in a language, just that it has probability p_1 of being randomly drawn.

   Then $d_{\mathcal{D}}(G_H, G_T) = \Pr_{\mathcal{D}}(x \in \mathbb{L}(G) \oplus \mathbb{L}(H))$. In words, this is the total mass of probability of the misclassified strings.

   For example, suppose $L_T = \{a^n b^n : n \in \mathbb{N}\}$ and we use the following distribution over $\Sigma^\star : \Pr_{\mathcal{D}}(u) = \frac{1}{2^{2|u|+1}}$. Now if $L_H = \varnothing$, we have $d_{\mathcal{D}}(G_H, G_T) = \Pr_{\mathcal{D}}(L_T) = \sum_{i \in \mathbb{N}} \frac{1}{2^{4i+1}} = \frac{1}{2} \sum_{i \in \mathbb{N}} \left(\frac{1}{16}\right)^i = \frac{8}{15}$.
   If $L_H = \{a^n b^n : n > 0\}$, $d_{\mathcal{D}}(G_H, G_T) = \Pr_{\mathcal{D}}(\lambda) = \frac{1}{2}$.

- G_T is a probabilistic grammar. In this case the examples are drawn following the distribution defined by the grammar itself. $\Pr_{G_T}$ and $\Pr_{G_H}$ denote the probability functions using the target grammar and (respectively) the hypothesis grammar. A number of alternative distances have been proposed:

  - $d_\infty(G_T, G_H) = \max_{x \in \Sigma^\star} |\Pr_{G_T}(x) - \Pr_{G_H}(x)|$

  - $d_k(G_T, G_H) = \left(\sum_{x \in \Sigma^\star}(|\Pr_{G_T}(x) - \Pr_{G_H}(x)|^k)\right)^{\frac{1}{k}}$

  - $\text{KL}(G_T, G_H) = \sum_{x \in \Sigma^\star} \Pr_{G_T}(x) \log(\Pr_{G_T}(x) / \Pr_{G_H}(x))$.

The Kullback and Leibler [1951] (KL) divergence is not a distance but it measures the cross-entropy between the target grammar and the hypothesis.

Definition 2.1   Let G_T be the target grammar and G_H a hypothesis grammar. Let $\epsilon > 0$. We say that G_H is an ϵ-good hypothesis w.r.t. G for distance d if$_{def}$ $d(G_T, G_H) < \epsilon$.

A learning algorithm is now asked to build a grammar given a *confidence* parameter δ and an *error* parameter ϵ. The algorithm is also given an upper bound n on the size of the target grammar and (sometimes) an upper bound m on the length of the examples it is going to get. The algorithm can query an oracle for an example randomly drawn according to the distribution $\mathcal{D}$. The query of an example or a counter-example will be denoted Ex(). When the oracle is only queried for a positive example, we will write Pos-Ex(). And when the oracle is only queried for strings of length $\leq m$, we will write Ex(m) and Pos-Ex(m), respectively. Formally, the oracle will then return a string drawn from $\mathcal{D}$, or $\mathcal{D}(\mathbb{L}(G))$, or $\mathcal{D}(\Sigma^{\leq m})$, or $\mathcal{D}(\mathbb{L}(G) \cap \Sigma^{\leq m})$, respectively, where $\mathcal{D}(L)$ is the restriction of $\mathcal{D}$ to the strings of L: $\mathrm{Pr}_{\mathcal{D}(L)}(x) = \mathrm{Pr}_{\mathcal{D}}(x) / \mathrm{Pr}_{\mathcal{D}}(L)$ if $x \in L$, 0 otherwise. $\mathrm{Pr}_{\mathcal{D}(L)}(x)$ is not defined if $L = \varnothing$.

Definition 2.2 (Polynomial PAC-learnability for discriminant grammars)   Let $\mathcal{G}$ be a class of grammars. $\mathcal{G}$ is PAC-learnable if_{def} there exists an algorithm $\mathcal{A}$ s.t. $\forall \epsilon, \delta > 0$, for any distribution $\mathcal{D}$ over $\Sigma^{\star}$, $\forall n \in \mathbb{N}$, $\forall G \in \mathcal{G}$ of size $\leq n$, for any upper bound $m \in \mathbb{N}$ on the size of the examples, if $\mathcal{A}$ has access to Ex(), ϵ, δ, n, and m, then with probability larger than $1 - \delta$, $\mathcal{A}$ returns an ϵ-good hypothesis w.r.t. G. If $\mathcal{A}$ runs in time polynomial in $\frac{1}{\epsilon}$, $\frac{1}{\delta}$, n, and m, we say that $\mathcal{G}$ is *polynomially* PAC-*learnable*.

In the case where the goal is to learn probabilistic grammars, the restriction on the length of the strings is meaningless and the definition is adapted as follows.

Definition 2.3 (Polynomial PAC-learnability for probabilistic grammars)   Let $\mathcal{G}$ be a class of probabilistic grammars. $\mathcal{G}$ is PAC-learnable if_{def} there exists an algorithm $\mathcal{A}$ s.t. $\forall \epsilon, \delta > 0$, $\forall n \in \mathbb{N}$, $\forall G \in \mathcal{G}$ of size $\leq n$, if $\mathcal{A}$ has access to Ex(), ϵ, δ, n then with probability larger than $1 - \delta$, $\mathcal{A}$ returns an ϵ-good hypothesis w.r.t. G (and the intended distance). If $\mathcal{A}$ runs in time polynomial in $\frac{1}{\epsilon}$, $\frac{1}{\delta}$, and n, we say that $\mathcal{G}$ is *polynomially* PAC-*learnable*.

Main Learning Results

The PAC-learnability of grammars from strings of unbounded size has always posed technical difficulties. Most results are negative [Kearns and Valiant 1989, Warmuth 1989, Kearns and Vazirani 1994].

When learning probabilistic automata, PAC-learning is the dominant setting. One of the reasons for this is that the identification in the limit with probability one has not allowed any satisfying definition regarding complexity issues [de la Higuera and Oncina 2004]. For different types of distances, PAC-learning algorithms have been proposed for deterministic probabilistic automata from text [Clark and Thollard 2004, Palmer and Goldberg 2005, Castro and Gavaldà 2008], with queries [Balle et al. 2010], and from data streams [Balle et al. 2014b].

A related independent question is that of computing the distances between distributions, i.e., between the probabilistic grammars or automata which define these. Interestingly, for PFA some distances are tractable while others are not, whereas for probabilistic context-free grammars, no distance can be computed [Lyngsø and Pedersen 2002, Nederhof and Satta 2004, de la Higuera et al. 2014].

2.3   GRAMMAR FORMALISMS

In many grammatical inference situations, the class of grammars is imposed. But there are also several situations where a careful analysis of the data and the goals of the task may allow one to choose the hypothesis class. The choice of the class is obviously crucial to success in learning: a discriminant model may be better than a probabilistic one; a simpler model (which will represent poorer structures) might do the job as well as a more complex one and, furthermore, be easier to learn.

In this section we present some of the most important classes of grammars and automata. In order to help the reader to choose the right type of grammars, we will, in each case, measure the capacity of a grammar (or automaton from that class) to do each of the following:

To parse: How easy is it, given an input string, to obtain the expected output?

To model: What grammatical structures can, or cannot, be modeled by using a grammar from this class?

To learn: Do we have learning algorithms (or, on the other hand, theoretical negative results)?

Complete formal definitions can be found in a number of textbooks; we choose here to present the models informally and rely principally on examples.

2.3.1   FINITE-STATE MACHINES RECOGNIZING STRINGS

Finite-state automata are used to decide if a string belongs to a language or not. A finite-state automaton is built using states and transitions between states. These transitions are labeled by symbols from the chosen (input) alphabet. A particular state is chosen as initial state (but there can be more than one if the automaton is non-deterministic); certain states are marked as final or accepting states. An automaton recognizes a string if there is a path of transitions leading from an initial state to a final state which *reads* this string. The language recognized by the automaton is exactly the set of strings recognized by it. We build upon the definitions from Section 1.6.

Deterministic Finite-State Automata

The language $\mathbb{L}_A$ *recognized* by the automaton $\mathcal{A}$ is the set of all strings x for which there exists a path leading from the initial state to a final state which reads string x. In the example represented in Figure 2.1, a is in $\mathbb{L}_A$, whereas ab is not. This machine is deterministic in the following sense: (1) there is just one initial state and (2) in every state, when having to read any symbol, there is at most one admissible transition.

Parsing with a DFA is straightforward and can be done in time linear in the length of the string to be parsed.

DFA admit a minimum canonical form, unique up to the names of the states. This has important consequences: equivalence can be tested in polynomial time.

Table 2.1 summarizes the parsing, modeling, and learning criteria for DFA.

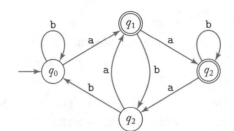

FIGURE 2.1: Graphical representation of a DFA.

TABLE 2.1: Deterministic finite-state automata: DFA

Criterion	Comment
Parsing	Parsing a string of length m can be done easily in time linear in m.
Modeling	A DFA can be used to recognize any regular language.
Learning	There are algorithms to learn DFA from an informant (from both examples and counter-examples). But to learn from positive examples only, extra bias is needed: the class of DFA (and therefore of languages) has to be reduced. Study of DFA learning has been very extensive with algorithms, in the active setting [Angluin 1988b], or from an informant [Oncina and García 1992]. In order to obtain positive learning results one can consider subclasses of the regular languages, leading to constrained types of deterministic finite automata: k-reversible languages admit automata which, when reversed, use a look-ahead of size k to parse [Angluin 1982], and k-testable languages are defined by legal and illegal substrings of length k [García and Vidal 1990].

Non-Deterministic Finite-State Automata

In a non-deterministic finite-state automaton (NFA), more freedom is allowed, since there may be different initial states and, from any particular state and any symbol, there may be several states reachable when reading a string. In the case of the NFA represented in Figure 2.2, this means that there are various parses for a particular string. For instance, string aa has three parses, two of which reach a final accepting state.

NFA can even have λ-transitions: these allow to move *freely* from one state to another. This is represented in Figure 2.3: with λ-transitions parsing becomes even more complex. But these λ-transitions can be removed with a polynomial-time algorithm.

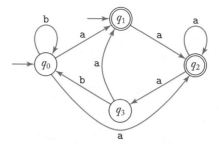

FIGURE 2.2: An NFA.

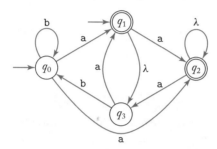

FIGURE 2.3: An NFA with λ-transitions. Some strings admit an infinity of parses.

NFA also suffer from some algorithmic inconveniences.

- Checking if two NFA are equivalent is $\mathcal{P}$-space complete. $\mathcal{A}$ and $\mathcal{B}$ are equivalent if_{def} they recognize the same language, i.e., if $\mathbb{L}_{\mathcal{A}} = \mathbb{L}_{\mathcal{B}}$.

- Minimizing an NFA is an $\mathcal{NP}$-hard problem. This is linked with the fact that there is no simple tractable normal or canonical form for NFA.[4]

Table 2.2 summarizes the parsing, modeling, and learning criteria for NFA.

Regular Expressions

These are used to describe languages in a linear (non-graphic) way using the symbols of the alphabet Σ and $+$ (indicating the union) and $*$ (for the iteration). The formal definitions are found in Definition 1.8.

---

4. In complexity theory, an $\mathcal{NP}$-hard problem is the hardest in the class of problems solvable in polynomial time by a non-deterministic Turing machine. More practically, the hypothesis $\mathcal{P} \neq \mathcal{NP}$ is generally believed to be true; as a consequence, an $\mathcal{NP}$-hard problem does not admit a tractable algorithm.

TABLE 2.2: Non-deterministic finite-state automata: NFA

Criterion	Comment
Parsing	Parsing a string of length m with an NFA of n states can be done in time in $\mathcal{O}(mn)$.
Modeling	A NFA can be used to recognize any regular language. But in certain cases the smallest DFA equivalent with a given NFA can be exponentially larger. Furthermore, there is no *natural* notion of *canonical* form, which also corresponds to the fact that there is no straightforward semantics.
Learning	There are few positive results concerning learning NFA. When algorithms exist, they will learn NFA corresponding to a subclass of the regular languages or have a complexity function of that of the corresponding smallest DFA.

TABLE 2.3: Regular expressions

Criterion	Comment
Parsing	Parsing a string with a regular expression typically requires transforming the regular expression into an NFA. The transformation can be expensive.
Modeling	Regular expressions model again the regular languages, like the DFA. But they can appear as *natural* modeling tools, for example in web applications, where XPATH expressions are tree-like extensions of regular expressions.
Learning	There are few positive results concerning learning regular expressions. One exception is by Fernau [2005], who attempts to learn these directly. In text extraction applications, heuristics allowing to find representing regular expressions have been proposed.

Example 2.2 aba*b(a + b)* is a regular expression. abb, ababaa are strings belonging to the language denoted by this regular expression. On the other hand, abaaa is not in the language.

Table 2.3 summarizes the parsing, modeling, and learning criteria for regular expressions.

2.3.2   PROBABILISTIC FINITE-STATE MACHINES

In the previous formalisms, parsing corresponds to answering the following question: Does this (candidate) string belong or not to the language? All strings in the language have equal importance. An alternative is to weigh the strings depending on their importance, which leads to the introduction of *weighted automata*. A variant of these where all weights are positive and the sum of total weights equals 1 leads to probabilistic languages. These can be recognized or generated, for example, by automata, hidden Markov models, or probabilistic context-free grammars.

Probabilistic Finite-State Automata

Probabilistic finite automata (PFA) are generative devices: they are built from a DFA or NFA structure, upon which three functions are added:

- $\mathbb{I}_{\mathbb{P}} : Q \rightarrow \mathbb{R}^+ \cap [0, 1]$ (initial probabilities);

- $\mathbb{F}_{\mathbb{P}} : Q \rightarrow \mathbb{R}^+ \cap [0, 1]$ (final probabilities); and

- $\delta_{\mathbb{P}} : Q \times (\Sigma \cup \{\lambda\}) \times Q \rightarrow \mathbb{R}^+$ is a transition function; the function is complete: $\mathbb{I}_{\mathbb{P}}$, $\delta_{\mathbb{P}}$, and $\mathbb{F}_{\mathbb{P}}$ are functions such that

$$\sum_{q \in Q} \mathbb{I}_{\mathbb{P}}(q) = 1, \tag{2.1}$$

and $\forall q \in Q$,

$$\mathbb{F}_{\mathbb{P}}(q) + \sum_{a \in \Sigma \cup \{\lambda\}, q' \in Q} \delta_{\mathbb{P}}(q, a, q') = 1. \tag{2.2}$$

The above definition is inspired by Vidal et al. [2005] and de la Higuera [2010]. A historical landmark is Paz [1971]. Let $x \in \Sigma^\star$, $\Pi_A(x)$ be the set of all paths accepting x: a path is a sequence $\pi = q_{i_0} x_1 q_{i_1} x_2 \ldots x_n q_{i_n}$ where $x = x_1 \cdots x_n$, $x_i \in \Sigma \cup \{\lambda\}$, and $\forall j \leq n$, $\exists p_j \neq 0$ such that $\delta_{\mathbb{P}}(q_{i_{j-1}}, x_j, q_{i_j}) = p_j$. The probability of the path π is

$$\mathbb{I}_{\mathbb{P}}(q_{i_0}) \cdot \prod_{j \in [n]} p_j \cdot \mathbb{F}_{\mathbb{P}}(q_{i_n}).$$

And the probability of the string x is obtained by summing over all the paths in $\Pi_A(x)$. Note that this may result in an infinite sum because of λ-transitions (and more problematically λ-cycles). An effective computation can be done by means of the FORWARD (or BACKWARD) algorithm [Vidal et al. 2005].

A PFA is represented in Figure 2.4; note that in some nodes, two probabilities are given—the one that the state is initial, and the one of halting in that state. The probability of a given string is taken by summing over the different accepting paths. On each path, the weights are multiplied. In Figure 2.5 there are λ-transitions. Since furthermore there is a cycle of λ-transitions this means that parsing is complex. It should be noted that even if PFA cannot be determinized in the way NFA can, there are algorithms to eliminate the λ-transitions.

Table 2.4 summarizes the parsing, modeling, and learning criteria for PFA.

Hidden Markov Models

Hidden Markov models (HMMs) [Rabiner 1989, Jelinek 1998] are finite-state machines defined by (1) a finite set of states, (2) a probabilistic transition function, (3) a distribution over initial states, and (4) an output function.

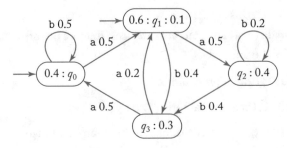

FIGURE 2.4: A PFA.

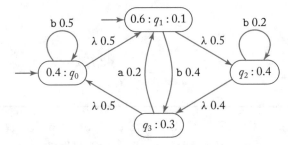

FIGURE 2.5: A PFA with λ-transitions.

An HMM generates a string by visiting (in a hidden way) states and outputting values when in those states. An HMM is represented in Figure 2.6:

- a state denoted $0.6 : q_2 : (a, 0.5)(b, 0.5)$ has probability 0.6 of being chosen as initial, and when reached will generate a and b with probability 0.5; and

- the weight labeling a transition initiating in state q indicates the probability of following this transition, when in state q.

Typical problems include finding the most probable path corresponding to a particular output (usually solved by the VITERBI algorithm).

Note that in order to obtain a distribution over $\Sigma^\star$ and not each Σ^m, one solution is to introduce a unique final state in which, once reached, the machine halts. An alternative often used is to introduce a special symbol (♯) and to only consider the strings terminating with ♯: the distribution is then defined over $\Sigma^\star ♯$. The HMM from Figure 2.6 is transformed into the one represented in Figure 2.7.

Equivalence results between HMMs and PFA can be found in Vidal et al. [2005].

Table 2.5 summarizes the parsing, modeling, and learning criteria for HMMs.

TABLE 2.4: Probabilistic finite-state automata: PFA

Criterion	Comment
Parsing	Parsing a string of length m with a PFA of n states can be done in time in $\mathcal{O}(mn^2)$ using the FORWARD algorithm.
Modeling	The deterministic restriction (DPFA) corresponds to a less powerful class: some distributions can be represented by PFA, but not by DPFA.
Learning	There are few theoretical positive results concerning learning PFA. The typical algorithm is EM (called BAUM-WELCH [Baum et al. 1970, Hulden 2012] in this setting): it starts with a particular structure and an initial setting of the parameters, then, iteratively, parses the strings from a sample and counts how the transitions are used, then updates the weights accordingly. For the special class of DPFA, there have been a number of algorithms, built on the state-merging techniques [Carrasco and Oncina 1994, Ron et al. 1995, Thollard et al. 2000, Clark and Thollard 2004]. The PAUTOMAC competition, which took place in 2012, was won by Shibata and Yoshinaka [2014]. Bayesian model-merging [Stolcke 1994] and spectral methods [Bailly 2011] are some other methods used for this task. A complete presentation of the PAUTOMAC findings can be found in Verwer et al. [2014].

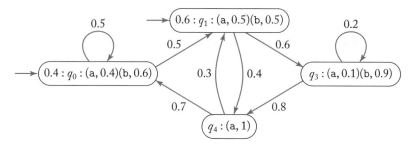

FIGURE 2.6: An HMM.

2.3.3 TRANSDUCERS

Transducers take strings as inputs, but also as outputs; they allow one to recognize bi-languages, and can also include weights.

Finite-State Transducers

Transducers are used for a number of tasks, including morphology [Roark and Sproat 2007] and automatic translation [Amengual et al. 2001]. A transducer is a finite-state machine in which there is not only an input but also an output string. Typically, outputs can be emitted both at the transitions and the final states.

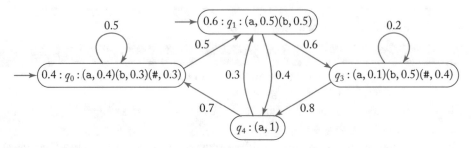

FIGURE 2.7: An HMM using ♯ to terminate the generation of strings. It defines a distribution over $\Sigma^\star \sharp$, and therefore can be used also over $\Sigma^\star$.

TABLE 2.5: Hidden Markov models: HMM

Criterion	Comment
Parsing	Parsing a string of length m with an HMM of n states can be done in time in $\mathcal{O}(mn^2)$.
Modeling	An HMM does not have final states: it therefore defines a distribution over each Σ^n. Through careful encoding, they can define the same distributions as those modeled by PFA.
Learning	There are few theoretical results concerning learning HMM as the main algorithm is an expectation-maximization method [BAUM-WELCH; Baum et al. 1970] whose convergence is problematic. Other learning methods include spectral methods [Hsu et al. 2012] and Gibbs sampling [Gelfand and Smith 1990].

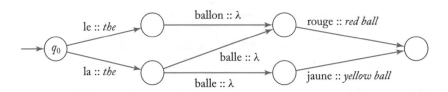

FIGURE 2.8: A rational transducer.

In Figure 2.8, we have represented a rational transducer, with outputs only on the transitions: we can use this transducer to find that the correct translation of input string "la balle rouge" is *"the red ball."*

Subsequential transducers are deterministic with respect to their input: this means that every input can only be translated into at most one output. Oncina et al. [1993] show that they are learnable

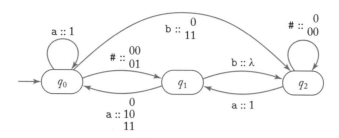

FIGURE 2.9: A semideterministic transducer.

when they describe *total functions*: every input string has exactly one translation. Vilar [1996] shows that they are learnable in an active setting by translation queries.

Extensions of this very constrained model exist: Allauzen and Mohri [2002] introduced p-subsequential transducers: these have multiple outputs at the states. Furthermore, machines for which inputs are deterministic but the outputs are not are called *semideterministic finite-state transducers* [Beros and de la Higuera 2014]. One such transducer is represented in Figure 2.9: given an input, there is at most one parse path, but there can be many different outputs.

On the other hand, general transducers can exist (with or without probabilities). They can be normalized in such a way that all transitions have labels of one of the following forms:

- input is a symbol, output is the empty string; and

- input is the empty string, output is a symbol.

In Figure 2.10 we have represented such a transducer. It can be seen that finding the possible output strings for a given input string is already a difficult question.

Table 2.6 summarizes the parsing, modeling, and learning criteria for transducers.

Probabilistic Finite-State Transducers

Weighted and probabilistic transducers are becoming increasingly popular. Weighted transducers have outputs that are weights and strings [Mohri 1997, Mohri et al. 2000].

Probabilistic finite-state transducers (PFST) are similar to PFA, but in this case two different alphabets (source Σ and target Γ) are involved. Each transition in a PFST has attached a symbol from the source alphabet (or λ) and a string (possible empty string) of symbols from the target alphabet. PFSTs can be viewed as graphs, as in Figure 2.11:

- a transition labeled b :: **00**, 0.2 will be followed with probability 0.2 and result in translating the input symbol b into the string **00**; and

- when reaching state q_2 there is probability 0.3 of halting.

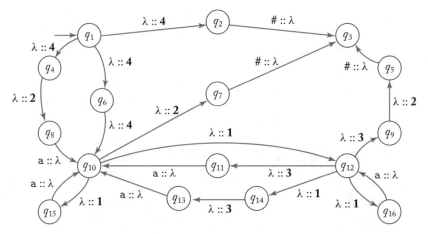

FIGURE 2.10: Normalized transducer.

TABLE 2.6: Transducers

Criterion	Comment
Parsing	In the context of transducers, parsing can lead to several different questions. If the question is that of checking whether y is a correct translation for x, this can be solved for general (non-deterministic) transducers in polynomial time. The question of discovering all the translations for a given input is ill-posed as the set can be infinite, even if it is a regular language; see Figure 2.10.
Modeling	Subsequential transducers only accept one translation for every input string, which is clearly a limitation. Extensions in which several possible outputs are allowed are the p-subsequential and semideterministic models.
Learning	Subsequential transducers can be learned from a sample [Oncina et al. 1993] or translation queries [Vilar 1996].

The transducer defines a distribution over bi-languages. One can note that the pair (ab, **110**) will be generated with probability $0.0036 = 0.3 \cdot 0.3 \cdot 0.2 \cdot 0.2$. More complex is the case of the pair (aa, **111**), which can be generated in two different ways. The probability of generating this pair is then $0.0135 = 0.3 \cdot 0.3 \cdot 0.3 \cdot 0.3 + 0.3 \cdot 0.3 \cdot 0.5 \cdot 0.4 \cdot 0.3$.

More formally, let $x \in \Sigma^\star$ and $y \in \Gamma^\star$. Let $\Pi_T(x, y)$ be the set of all paths accepting (x, y): a path is a sequence $\pi = q_{i_0}(x_1, y_1)q_{i_1}(x_2, y_2) \ldots (x_n, y_n)q_{i_n}$ where $x = x_1 \cdots x_n$ and $y = y_1 \cdots y_n$, with $\forall j \in [n]$, $x_j \in \Sigma \cup \{\lambda\}$ and $y_j \in \Gamma^\star$, and $\forall j \in [n]$, $\exists p_{i_j}$ such that $(q_{i_{j-1}}, x_j, y_j, q_{i_j}, p_{i_j}) \in E$. The probability of the path is

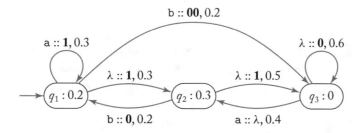

FIGURE 2.11: A probabilistic transducer.

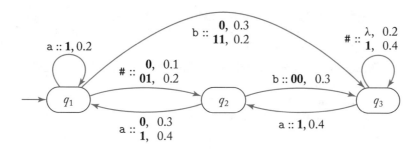

FIGURE 2.12: A probabilistic semideterministic transducer.

$$\mathbb{I}_{\mathbb{P}}(q_{i_0}) \cdot \prod_{j \in [n]} p_{i_j} \cdot \mathbb{F}_{\mathbb{P}}(q_{i_n}).$$

And the probability of the translation pair (x, y) is obtained by summing over all the paths in $\Pi_{\mathcal{T}}(x, y)$. The probability of y given x (the probability of y as a translation of x, denoted as $\Pr_{\mathcal{T}}(y|x)$) is $\frac{\Pr_{\mathcal{T}}(x, y)}{\sum_{z \in \Sigma^\star} \Pr_{\mathcal{T}}(x, z)}$.

The problem of finding the optimal translation is called *optimal decoding*: it is $\mathcal{NP}$-hard [Casacuberta and de la Higuera 2000]. Recent work provides techniques allowing to compute this string in many cases [de la Higuera and Oncina 2013]. Semideterministic transducers can also be adapted in order to include probabilities and define distributions over bi-languages, as in Figure 2.12.

Table 2.7 summarizes the parsing, modeling, and learning criteria for probabilistic transducers.

2.3.4 MORE COMPLEX FORMALISMS

Finite-state machines can only model certain languages. The different models we have surveyed can be rendered more complex in a number of ways.

TABLE 2.7: Probabilistic transducers

Criterion	Comment
Parsing	There are several parsing problems related to probabilistic transducers:
	• Computing $\Pr(x, y)$ can be done by adapting the FORWARD algorithm.
	• The *stochastic translation problem* of a source sentence is: given input string x, find a target string y that maximizes $\Pr(y \mid x)$ or $\Pr(x, y)$. In other words, we are looking for the most probable translation. This is actually a complex intractable problem [Casacuberta and de la Higuera 2000] for which a number of heuristics exist, and an efficient parameterized algorithm has been designed [de la Higuera and Oncina 2014].
Modeling	The expressiveness of probabilistic transducers depends on the amount of determinism allowed. There are some rich extensions allowing to define distributions: negative and even complex weights have been proposed.
Learning	There are few positive formal results concerning learning PST. In the identification in the limit line, Akram et al. [2012] learn the deterministic ones in an active setting and Akram and de la Higuera [2012] in a batch setting. In a PAC learning setting, recent results have been obtained by Balle et al. [2014a].

- General context-free grammars correspond to the second step of the Chomsky Hierarchy. They model languages which can also be recognized by push-down automata.

- Probabilistic context-free grammars are the probabilistic version of the above.

- Bi-grammars are context-free extensions of the transducers: the bi-languages are built by using context-free like rewriting rules.

- Whereas all these models deal with strings, there is in many cases a natural albeit technical extension to trees: tree automata, tree grammars, tree transducers, etc. In certain cases, graph languages can also be defined.

Context-Free Grammars

A context-free grammar is used to generate strings. It can be used for parsing by algorithms running in $\mathcal{O}(m^3)$ time, where m is the length of the string. The two better known algorithms for doing this are the Earley [1970] and the CYK [Younger 1967] algorithms.

It is often a sound policy to normalize the context-free grammars: when in Chomsky (or quadratic) normal form, the right hand of rules is of length at most 2; when in Greibach normal form, the right hands start with a terminal symbol. Grammatical inference specialists should be aware that when learning a normal form, the actual structure of the strings changes. If what matters

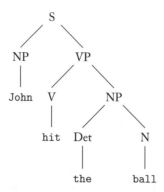

FIGURE 2.13: Parse tree for John hit the ball.

is only the language, this is not an issue. But if one is also interested in why a string belongs to the language, then one will need the derivation or parse tree which is grammar dependent and not language dependent.

One curious grammatical inference example illustrates this point: Sakakibara [1990] proves that *reversible grammars* are learnable from skeletons; skeletons are parse trees with no labels on the internal nodes of the tree. Furthermore, he shows that any context-free *language* admits a reversible normal form (even if the construction can be exponential). It would therefore seem natural to claim that context-free languages are learnable from skeletons. If so, this would represent great news as skeletons can easily be built from treebanks by just removing the labels of the internal nodes! The answer is nevertheless negative, as the sort of skeletons we would need to be able to use Sakakibara's result are not those that appear naturally when analyzing natural language. So the language inferred by this technique would be very far away from the natural language we would expect.

Example 2.3 The following grammar generates well-structured bracketed languages: $\langle \{N_1\}, \{a, b\}, N_1, R \rangle$ with $R = \{N_1 \to aN_1bN_1; N_1 \to \lambda\}$.

A typical parse tree for a context-free grammar that may be used for English is represented in Figure 2.13.

Linear grammars are context-free grammars in which right-hand sides of rules contain at most one non-terminal. The good news is that parsing strings using linear grammars is in $\mathcal{O}(n^2)$ time. The bad news is that there is no real advantage, as far as learnability is concerned, in using linear grammars: as discussed in Section 2.1.1, the equivalence problem remains undecidable, which is a barrier for learning. Nevertheless, there are some cases where learning is possible: even linear grammars [Takada 1988] and deterministic linear grammars [de la Higuera and Oncina 2002] have been shown to be learnable.

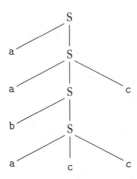

FIGURE 2.14: Parse tree for the sentence aabaccc for a linear grammar with rules $S \rightarrow aS|bS|aSc|acc$.

Example 2.4   In Figure 2.14 is an example of a linear grammar and of a tree.

Even linear grammars are those linear grammars where, on the right-hand side of the rules, the unique non-terminal symbol, if present, has, to its left and to its right, an identical number of terminal symbols. If such grammars are used, it is easy to find the center of a string and therefore to produce a *skeleton*. Therefore, learning such grammars is as difficult as learning finite-state machines.

Example 2.5 $\langle\{N_1\}, \{a, b\}, N_1, R\rangle$ with $R = \{N_1 \rightarrow aN_1a|bN_1b|a|b|\lambda\}$ is a linear grammar which generates palindromes. Furthermore, this grammar is even linear. Figure 2.15 shows a parse tree for this grammar.

Deterministic linear grammars were shown to be learnable by de la Higuera and Oncina [2002]. A probabilistic version is studied by de la Higuera and Oncina [2003]. In such grammars there is exactly one terminal symbol before the non-terminal in the right-hand side of the rules and there is a deterministic rule to be followed.

Example 2.6   The following is a deterministic linear grammar:

$$\langle\{N_1, N_2\}, \{a, b\}, N_1, R\rangle \text{ with } R = \{N_1 \rightarrow aN_1ab|bN_2; \ N_2 \rightarrow aN_1a|b\}.$$

Table 2.8 summarizes the parsing, modeling, and learning criteria for CFGS.

Probabilistic Context-Free Grammars

Definition 2.4   A *probabilistic context-free grammar (PCFG)* G is a quintuple $\langle V, \Sigma, N, R, P \rangle$ where V is a finite alphabet (of variables or non-terminals), Σ is a finite alphabet (of terminal symbols), N $(\in V)$ is the start symbol, $R \subset V \times (V \cup \Sigma)^*$ is a finite set of production rules, and $P : R \rightarrow \mathbb{R}^+$ is the probability function. Furthermore, (1) $\forall r \in R, 0 < P(r) \leq 1$ and (2) $\forall A \in N, \sum (A, \alpha) \in R : P(A, \alpha) = 1$.

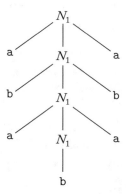

FIGURE 2.15: Parse tree for an even linear grammar.

TABLE 2.8: Context-free grammars

Criterion	Comment
Parsing	CYK and the Early algorithm are two parsing algorithms, both with cubic complexity.
Modeling	Context-free grammars allow for the representing of patterns which are not regular: palindromes and brackets, for instance.
Learning	Sakakibara [1990] has proposed different learning results from bracketed data. In unsupervised learning, there are no efficient algorithms, one exception being an active learning result [Clark 2010a]. But a number of alternative approaches have been studied. Some of these are presented in Chapter 4.

A PCFG is used to generate strings by rewriting iteratively the non-terminals in the string, beginning with the start symbol. A string may be obtained by different derivations. In this case the problem is called ambiguity. Parsing with a PCFG is usually done by transforming the PCFG into one equivalent in quadratic normal form and adapting the Earley or the CYK algorithms.

Table 2.9 summarizes the parsing, modeling, and learning criteria for PCFGs.

Bigrammars

Translation tasks requiring rules that cannot be described through finite-state machines mechanisms can make use of a formalism associating context-free grammars and transducers. A *synchronous grammar* (or synchronous phrase structure grammar) is made of a set of rules of the form $T \rightarrow$ input ; output where T is a non-terminal, input is a string over non-terminals and labeled terminal

TABLE 2.9: Probabilistic context-free grammars

Criterion	Comment
Parsing	CYK and the Early algorithm are two parsing algorithms which can be adapted to work with probabilistic context-free grammars. A very efficient extension of the Early algorithm due to Stolcke [1995], which can compute: • the probability of a given string x generated by a PCFG G; • the single most probable parse for x; • the probability that x occurs as a prefix of some string generated by G.
Modeling	Context-free grammars allow us to represent patterns which are not regular: palindromes and brackets, for instance.
Learning	There are two issues when contemplating learning PCFGs. Unsupervised learning is the task consisting of learning these from just strings. Alternatives are to start with very general grammars and attempt to estimate the parameters. This can be done with the inside-outside algorithm [Lari and Young 1990]. Bayesian methods will rely on priors: a knowledge of some characteristics concerning the distribution which will help the algorithm to converge. Algorithm COMINO produces interesting results [Scicluna and de la Higuera 2014b]. The supervised task is simpler, as it consists of learning from the treebank.

symbols from the input alphabet, and output is a string over non-terminals and labeled terminal symbols from the output alphabet.

A typical rule might be

$$NP \rightarrow \texttt{el libro grande ; the big book}$$

$$NP \rightarrow \texttt{el } NOUN_1 \ ADJ_2 \text{ ; the } ADJ_2 \ NOUN_1.$$

Notice that only a one-to-one mapping is allowed. Parsing with such machines can be complex. A natural extension consist in adding probabilities to the rules [Koehn 2010].

2.3.5   DEALING WITH TREES AND GRAPHS

Strings and sequences represent the first level of structured information. In a number of applications much more information (and of a much richer nature) can be represented through trees or even graphs. The learning problems will obviously be harder, but the benefits will be higher.

The theories of tree automata and graph grammars are out of the scope of this book. However, here we name just a few:

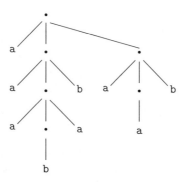

FIGURE 2.16: Skeleton corresponding to the bracketed string (a(a(a(b)a)b)(a(a)b)).

- If one chooses only to bracket a sentence, the result may be represented as a skeleton. A skeleton is a tree in which the internal nodes are unlabeled. See Example 2.7 for the simple idea.

- Trees will usually be ordered, and the internal nodes of a tree will be marked by valuable labels. This is the case of the trees one can find produced by a parser for natural language. Tree grammars and automata have been thoroughly studied in the past [Comon et al. 1997].

- Graphs can be directed or not. Graphs will possibly represent complex dependencies between the constituents of a sentence. Graph grammars have been studied in detail [Courcelle and Engelfriet 2012]. When asked to be learnable, the grammars have to be simplified [Oates et al. 2002, 2003].

Example 2.7   An example of a skeleton is depicted in Figure 2.16.

2.4   IS GRAMMATICAL INFERENCE AN INSTANCE OF MACHINE LEARNING?

As grammatical inference deals with learning automata and grammars, the reader familiar with machine learning will be interested in relating some key machine learning concepts with grammatical inference. Interestingly, both natural language processing and machine learning were discussed by Turing [1950] in his work about *machine intelligence*: he worked on both and partially reported some of his findings.

Nowadays, machine learning is a well-established field of research, with its journals, conferences, companies, and teams. It also has a theory of its own which is studied in universities throughout the world. This theory is based on some profound statistically inspired work by Vapnik and Chervonenkis [1971] and some more combinatorially inspired work by Valiant [1984].

Vapnik's approach is to characterize the learning problem as one of studying convergence issues regarding the *empirical risk*. The empirical risk measures the errors made when finding a hypothesis explaining the examples. There are then two sources of errors: a first one concerns the fact that the optimization process may not return the real optimum, and the second concerns the fact that the set of hypotheses may not be able to capture exactly what has to be learned. Vapnik studies how the generalization risk (measuring the errors to be made on unseen data) will converge to the empirical risk.

In Valiant's framework (see Section 2.2.6), we suppose that what is to be learned does belong to the hypothesis space. We will then ask if it is possible to explore efficiently this space and return a consistent hypothesis in this space.

Since grammatical inference is seen by many as a particular form of machine learning, one may believe that it is sufficient to adapt the above well-studied theories to the setting of grammatical inference. In general, this approach does not work well; here are some simple reasons for this.

- In classical machine learning, a good measure of the hypotheses class is the VC-dimension (Vapnik–Chervonenkis). The VC-dimension of the class expresses how easy it is to find a hypothesis that will match a given set of examples and counter-examples. A small VC-dimension will usually mean that the class of hypotheses is poor, which in turn means that a good hypothesis inside the class is going to be hard to better. A high VC-dimension means that the class is rich and that finding a consistent hypothesis is always possible: this encourages overfitting and will usually result in hardness results, because of the high variance.

  Mathematically, the VC-dimension is the size of the largest set which can be shattered by the hypothesis class; a set $X = \{x_1, x_2, \ldots, x_n\}$ is shattered by a class $\mathcal{H}$ if given any partition of X into X_1 and X_2 there is a hypothesis h in $\mathcal{H}$ which classifies all elements of X_1 as 1, and all those of X_2 as 0.

  But the VC-dimension for typical classes of automata or grammars is infinite. This is easy to see: if we are given any finite language, in most formalisms it is possible to build an infinity of automata or grammars which recognize/generate exactly the strings from the finite language. A usual way around this is to restrict the class by indexing it by the size of the grammars it contains. The new question is then: What is the VC-dimension for the automata with at most n states, or for the grammars with at most n rules? Here again, the results are disappointing, with VC-dimensions of $\mathcal{O}(n \log n)$ for DFA and $\mathcal{O}(n^2)$ for NFA: such results are inconclusive and do not allow one to derive the sort of bounds for which one would hope.

- Traditional computational learning tools will prove that finding consistent DFA is a hard problem, as hard as a number of cryptographic problems [Kearns and Vazirani 1994]. This in turn results in not allowing for positive PAC learning results.

2.5   SUMMARY

To conclude this chapter, let us ask ourselves how theoretical results can help.

The first thing to understand is that a first decision people attempting to build a learning system have to make is what sort of grammar they are thinking of learning. This is going to constitute the *learning bias*. Indeed, the learner is not just trying to learn from data: it has to decide what biased solution it is looking for. More generally, the bias-variance trade-off issue (or the related one of *no free lunch*) is very present in grammatical inference and is an issue to be taken seriously!

This may seem frustrating. After all, why not let the learning system find an unbiased grammar? There are many works in learning theory showing that this naive approach is doomed. It is always possible to find a very complex grammar consistent with the data, provided this data is non-contradictory.

And the choice of grammars will depend on our understanding of what we are looking for, of the sort of essential rules governing the structure of sentences or words. But also on our understanding of how grammars model languages, of how easy they are to learn.

The second question we will want to raise is that of the learning paradigm. In the *real* learning situation we are to face, the way we receive the data, the way it is generated, and the properties of this matter will all be elements important to analyze. The theoretical tools from grammatical inference allow us to do that.

Obviously, the fact that our learning algorithm has nice positive convergence properties will not ensure that learning will be possible when facing a specific learning situation. But curiously, there still is an advantage of having some theorem telling us that the algorithms the learner is using can learn or identify some unknown targets, although not all. Consider the significance of the assessment "this class is not learnable." If a class is not learnable, this means that somewhere in the class there are some targets which are not learnable. It means that if what we were hoping to learn was one of those targets, then we should forget it or rely on luck. Going further, this signifies that if we divide the class of grammars under scrutiny into the subclass of the ones the algorithm can learn and the subclass of those the algorithm cannot learn, there is in fact a *hidden bias*: the real class our algorithm is learning is probably quite different from the class we intend to learn from.

In other words, we say that we are using bias A but are really using bias B. The worse part is that usually we cannot know what B is!

CHAPTER 3

Learning Regular Languages

3.1 INTRODUCTION

This chapter primarily examines how regular patterns can be learned from positive data. It also emphasizes an approach to learning by selecting the bias carefully. This is because many of the important, practical grammatical inference techniques were developed in this way. It is also because many of the insights obtained here can be, have been, and continue to be fruitfully applied to non-regular classes. And so there is every reason to believe that the lessons here are valuable in ongoing research on language learning.

The first section of this chapter explains why appropriately selected bias is a valuable way to attend to learning problems in computational linguistics. As explained there, it is not the only way, and others have and continue to be pursued.

The main learning technique discussed in this chapter is state-merging. State-merging will be introduced in terms of learning regular sets (i.e., regular languages), although we will also see that state-merging is used to learn regular relations and probabilistic regular languages as well. Regular sets are used to exemplify the algorithms because they are simpler and more well studied.

State-merging itself is introduced with respect to an example problem in the acquisition of phonology. The concrete example is intended to help exposition. The state-merging theorem (Theorem 3.2), which establishes the soundness of the method, is also presented.

This chapter then discusses RPNI, an algorithm which *efficiently* learns *any* regular language from positive *and negative* data in the sense discussed in the previous chapter. RPNI is included because it reinforces the utility of the state-merging theorem (Theorem 3.2) and the importance of canonical forms as learning targets, and because the idea behind it underlies successful algorithms, which learn classes stochastic languages and regular transductions.

These other algorithms for learning regular relations and stochastic regular languages are also discussed, although in less detail. The chapter concludes with suggestions for further reading.

3.2   BIAS SELECTION REDUCES THE PROBLEM SPACE

Natural language patterns fall across different regions of the Chomsky Hierarchy. When trying to understand how such patterns could be learned, there are generally two different strategies that have been adopted.

One strategy is to define learning so that increasingly larger regions can be learned. An important idea in this line of work is that different learning frameworks may better characterize the data presentations learners actually get. For example, in the framework *identification in the limit from positive data*, the class of data presentations with which learners must succeed has been criticized as being too broad, antagonistic, and unrealistic [Clark and Lappin 2011]. Frameworks in which learners are able to learn large regions of the Chomsky Hierarchy succeed in no small part because they limit the data presentations with which learners must succeed in significant ways (e.g., to classes of computable data presentations) [Gold 1967, Horning 1969, Angluin 1988a]; see also the discussion in Heinz [2015]).

Another strategy is to identify learnable regions which cross-cut the Chomsky Hierarchy. The idea here is that important properties of natural language are overlooked by the major regions of the Chomsky Hierarchy, and by restricting the class of languages to be learned, the additional knowledge that comes with this target class can be harnessed to solve the learning problem. In the framework *identification in the limit from positive data*, this means the target class will have to exclude some finite languages [Gold 1967] and a defining property of such classes is provided by Angluin [1980]. Many examples of such classes have been studied in the grammatical inference literature.

Both these two strategies have a common theme at their core. The common theme is this: hard problems are easier to solve with better characterizations. This is because the instance space of the problem has been reduced in a meaningful way.

A simple example illustrates this general point. The Hamiltonian path problem is the problem of finding a path in an undirected graph which visits each node vertex in the graph exactly once. This problem is known to be $\mathcal{NP}$-complete [Garey and Johnson 1979]. However, if the graphs are restricted to linear sequences (like stations along a single rail line), the problem has a trivial solution. Note that in both the original and restricted versions of this problem, the instance space of the problem is countably infinite. But the restriction makes the problem solvable. As anticipated by Gold [1967], research in grammatical inference has shown that meaningful restrictions of either the class of data presentations or the class of languages that learners are required to succeed on can make the learning problem solvable.

This chapter focuses on state-merging, which exemplifies a sound way bias selection (the second strategy) can be instantiated in algorithms for learning regular languages.

3.3   REGULAR GRAMMARS

In this chapter, there are three kinds of patterns to be discussed: regular sets, regular relations, and regular distributions over sets or relations (i.e., regular stochastic sets or relations). Although there are many ways to define grammars for each of these types of patterns, they are defined here in terms of finite-state automata. One reason for this is that many kinds of finite-state automata admit canonical forms. Canonical forms are advantageous because they typically directly reflect invariant mathematical properties of the patterns they describe. Particular canonical forms for automata will be introduced shortly.[1] Another reason for using finite-state automata is that one of the main techniques for inferring regular grammars relies on the concept of merging the states of these automata; this technique is called *state-merging*.

Deterministic finite-state acceptors (DFA) were defined in Section 1.6. Non-deterministic finite-state acceptors (NFA) were introduced in Section 2.3.1. They are defined here both for completeness and so that we can precisely state important theorems later.

For any set of S, let $\mathcal{P}(S)$ denote the powerset of S (the set of all subsets of S).

Definition 3.1 (Non-deterministic finite-state acceptor (NFA))   A *non-deterministic finite-state acceptor* is a 5-tuple $\langle \Sigma, Q, I, F, \delta \rangle$ for which

- Σ is the finite set of input symbols, corresponding to the vocabulary;

- Q is a finite set of states;

- I is the finite set of initial states ($I \subseteq Q$);

- F is the finite set of final states ($F \subseteq Q$); and

- $\delta : Q \times \Sigma \to \mathcal{P}(Q)$ is the (total) transition function; given a state $q \in Q$ and input symbol $i \in \Sigma$, $\delta(q, i)$ returns a set of states $Q' \subseteq Q$.

The transition function is extended recursively so that its domain is $\mathcal{P}(Q) \times \Sigma^*$. Then the language generated, recognized, or accepted by a finite-state acceptor A is

$$\mathbb{L}(A) = \{w \in \Sigma^* \mid \delta(I, w) \cap F \neq \varnothing\}.$$

There are two important facts about the class of NFA. First, it properly includes the class of DFA. Thus deterministic acceptors are a special type of NFA. Second, the family of languages describable with NFA is exactly the same as the family of languages describable with DFA: it is the class of regular languages.

---

1. In contrast, there are no (computable in polynomial time) canonical (e.g., shortest) regular expressions for regular sets.

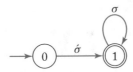

FIGURE 3.1: A finite-state acceptor which recognizes the language $\acute{\sigma}\sigma^*$.

We now wish to introduce two canonical forms of regular languages by way of an example. Consider $\Sigma = \{\acute{\sigma}, \grave{\sigma}, \sigma\}$. These symbols denote strongly stressed, weakly stressed, and unstressed syllables, respectively. Following the linguistic observation that words can have many weakly stressed syllables but (usually) at most one strongly stressed syllable, we will refer to the weakly stressed syllables as secondary stressed and the strongly stressed syllables as primary stressed syllables. Now consider the finite-state acceptor defined pictorially in Figure 3.1. The states are $Q = \{0, 1\}$; the initial state $\{0\}$; the final states $\{1\}$; and $\delta = \{(0,\acute{\sigma}) \mapsto \{1\}, (1,\sigma) \mapsto \{1\}\}$. Consequently, this acceptor recognizes the formal language containing all and only those strings which begin with the symbol $\acute{\sigma}$ and is then followed by zero or more σ symbols. In other words, this formal language represents a linguistic pattern in which the initial syllables bear the primary (strongest) stress and the other syllables are unstressed.

For every regular language L, there are infinitely many finite-state acceptors which recognize L. However, there is a particular acceptor for L, which is often called the canonical form. This acceptor is the smallest *deterministic* acceptor recognizing L.[2] An NFA is deterministic provided $|I| = 1$ and for all states $q \in Q$ and symbols $\sigma \in \Sigma$, it is the case that $|\delta(q, \sigma)| \leq 1$ (so there is at most one state reachable from q on reading σ).

An important fact about the canonical form of a regular language is that the states are intimately related to algebraic properties of the language. To explain, it is important to understand that, for every regular language L, every string $w \in \Sigma^*$ can be associated with a *residual* stringset, also called the set of *good tails*. The good tails (or residual) of w with respect to L are all strings v such that $wv \in L$. The good tails are all the ways in which w can be continued so that the resulting string belongs to L. Formally, $\text{Tails}_L(w) = \{v \mid wv \in L\}$. Consider the language of the NFA in Figure 3.1, which would be written with a regular expression as $\acute{\sigma}\sigma^*$. The good tails of $\acute{\sigma}\sigma$ with respect to this language is the set indicated by the regular expression σ^*. On the other hand, the good tails of $\sigma\acute{\sigma}$ with respect to this language is empty.

---

2. There are other canonical representations of regular languages, including the syntactic monoid [McNaughton and Papert 1971] and the universal automaton [Lombardy and Sakarovitch 2008].

Nerode and Myhill considered an equivalence relation over Σ^* induced by L: two strings w_1 and w_2 are L-equivalent if and only if they have the same set of good tails with respect to L. Continuing the example above, it is not difficult to verify that the strings $\acute{\sigma}\sigma$, $\acute{\sigma}\sigma\sigma$, and $\acute{\sigma}$ are all tail-equivalent with respect to the language $\acute{\sigma}\sigma^*$.

Nerode and Myhill proved that the L-tail-equivalence relation partitions Σ^* into finitely many blocks if and only if L is a regular language. An important result in their proof is that the states of the smallest deterministic acceptor recognizing L represent the blocks of this equivalence relation. In other words, for every canonical acceptor for a regular language, for every state q in this acceptor, every string which leads to q has exactly the same set of good tails. For this reason, the smallest DFA is also called the *tail canonical acceptor* for a regular language L.

In a completely symmetric fashion, one can define the suffixes of a string, the *heads* of a string with respect to a language, and a head-equivalence relation.[3] The Myhill–Nerode theorem is easily adapted to this other construction: the regular languages are exactly those for which the L-head-equivalence relation partitions Σ^* into finitely many blocks. The head canonical acceptor is in fact the smallest *reverse deterministic* acceptor for a regular language L. An acceptor is reverse deterministic provided it is deterministic if its reverse acceptor is deterministic. (The reverse NFA switches the start states with final states, and points the transitions in the other direction. Formally, for an NFA $A = \langle \Sigma, Q, I, F, \delta \rangle$, the reverse of A is $A^r = \langle \Sigma, Q, F, I, \delta^r \rangle$ where $\delta^r(q, i) = \{q' \mid q \in \delta(q', i)\}$.)

The head canonical acceptor and tail canonical acceptor have different structures, which reflect their right-to-left and left-to-right orientations, respectively. While the left-to-right orientation may appear more natural for production (since time moves "left to right"), there is a reason to think accessing strings right-to-left plays a role in cognition. If strings are stored in memory in a first-in/last-out fashion (like plates stacked on one of those cafeteria-style spring-based storage systems) then when accessing the string from memory, it will be read right-to-left.

These results for tail and head canonical acceptors are important for learning because it provides a way to distinguish or not distinguish the underlying states based on information present in the strings. If there is reason to believe that two observed prefixes (suffixes) w_1 and w_2 of a language have the same set of tails (heads), then those two prefixes (suffixes) will lead to the same state in the tail (head) canonical acceptor. On the other hand, if there is reason to believe w_1 and w_2 do not have the same set of tails (heads) then they should lead to different states in the tail (head) canonical acceptor. As we will see below, there can be reasons why two observed prefixes (suffixes) have the

---

3. Formally, v is a suffix of w iff there exists $u \in \Sigma^*$ such $w = uv$. The good heads of v with respect to L are all strings u such that $uv \in L$. Two strings v_1 and v_2 are L-head-equivalent if and only if they have the same set of good heads with respect to L.

same set of tails (heads) or not. This connection is made more explicit in Sections 3.5 and 3.6, below, after its mechanics are introduced.

3.4   STATE-MERGING ALGORITHMS

State-merging is a technique which refers to a class of algorithms. It will be emphasized that one way different state-merging algorithms can be obtained is by altering the criteria for deciding which states should be merged.

State-merging is a method of writing smaller and smaller finite-state descriptions of observed strings while keeping some property invariant. The general scheme of learners of this type follow a two-step procedure.

1. A finite-state representation of the input.

2. Merge states that are equivalent (in some predetermined sense).

Which finite-state representation of the input is used and how it is decided which states to merge in this structure are the two key questions involved when developing a state-merging algorithm. These decisions determine everything: the kinds of generalizations that are made, and ultimately the kinds of patterns which can be learned.

Below we first explain the process of merging states in a finite-state acceptor—what it is and how it works. Then we explain how the input to the learning algorithm can be represented as a finite-state acceptor. We conclude with the state-merging theorem, which establishes the soundness of this approach to learning to regular languages. The theorem is possible partly from the fact that there are canonical representations of regular languages. Along the way, we illustrate these ideas with examples, drawing in particular on a problem children face when learning the phonology of their native language.

3.4.1   THE PROBLEM OF LEARNING STRESS PATTERNS

Before continuing further, let us illustrate one problem in phonological acquisition which well help along the exposition regarding state-merging: the problem of learning the stress pattern of one's native language (if one exists) from syllabic representations of words.

Many languages have stress patterns. For example, consider the words in Pintupi shown in Table 3.1 [Hansen and Hansen 1969, p. 163]. If we abstract to the level of syllables, the pattern stands out more clearly, as shown in Table 3.2. Hayes [1995, p. 62] described the stress pattern of Pintupi as follows:

1. primary stress falls on the initial syllable, and

2. secondary stress falls on alternating non-final syllables.

TABLE 3.1: Pintupi words

a.	páŋa	"earth"
b.	tʲútaya	"many"
c.	máḻawàna	"through from behind"
d.	púḻiŋkàlatʲu	"we (sat) on the hill"
e.	tʲámulìmpatʲùŋku	"our relation"
f.	tíḻirìŋulàmpatʲu	"the fire for our benefit flared up"
g.	kúranʲùlulìmpatʲùɻa	"the first one who is our relation"
h.	yúmaɻìŋkamàratʲùɻɻaka	"because of mother-in-law"

TABLE 3.2: Pintupi words with a syllabic representation

a. σ́σ	e. σ́σσ̀σσ
b. σ́σσ	f. σ́σσ̀σσσ
c. σ́σσ̀σ	g. σ́σσ̀σσ̀σσ
d. σ́σσ̀σσ	h. σ́σσ̀σσ̀σσσ

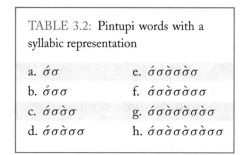

FIGURE 3.2: A minimal, deterministic, finite-state acceptor for Pintupi stress.

These generalizations can be encoded as a finite-state acceptor, as shown in Figure 3.2.

Here is a different example of a stress pattern found in the world's languages: the unbounded stress pattern in Kwakwala [Walker 2000]:

1. Primary stress falls on the left-most heavy syllable in a word, and if there are no heavy syllables, it falls on the final syllable.

TABLE 3.3: All LHOR words up to four syllables in length

Ĥ	Ĺ	ĤL	ĤH	LĤ
LĹ	ĤLL	ĤLH	ĤHL	ĤHH
LĤL	LĤH	LLĹ	LLĤ	LĤLL
LĤLH	ĤLLL	ĤLLH	ĤHLL	ĤHLH
LĤHL	LĤHH	ĤLHL	ĤLHH	ĤHHL
ĤHHH	LLĤL	LLĤH	LLLĹ	LLLĤ

Many languages, like Kwakwala, distinguish between "light" and "heavy" syllables. The "weight" of a syllable can be determined by vowel length, presence of a coda, and potentially many other factors [Gordon 2006].

Following Hayes [1995], we refer to this pattern as the "Leftmost Heavy Otherwise Rightmost" (LHOR) pattern. According to this generalization, in words with syllable profiles LLH, LLHL, and LLHLH, the primary stress will always fall on the third syllable because that is the leftmost heavy syllable in each word.[4] Table 3.3 shows all words up to four syllables in length which exemplify this pattern. This pattern is unbounded because the primary stress could fall arbitrarily far from either word edge. For example, in words with the syllable profile LLLHLLH, stress is predicted to fall on the fourth syllable. On the other hand, according to the rule, a word with only light syllables will have stress fall on the final syllable of the word (as in LLLLĹ).

Just as with the Pintupi, it is important to realize that the generalizations above apply equally well to longer words, even if no such words of that length exist in the lexicon (or are constructible by word formation rules). The words in Table 3.3 are just among the shortest words drawn from this set. Letting $\Sigma = \{H, Ĥ, L, Ĺ\}$, the finite-state acceptor in Figure 3.3 describes this infinite set, and thus captures the linguistic generalization faithfully.

More generally, the linguistic generalizations that phonologists make when describing the dominant stress patterns in languages can be thought of as infinite sets. Our interest in the nature of these phonological generalizations leads us to examine the nature of these mathematical objects—the infinite sets with which these generalizations are identified.

These examples are introduced in order to concretely establish the nature of the learning problem. What algorithm can take the finite sets of data in Tables 3.2 and 3.3 as input and output the finite-state acceptors in Figures 3.2 and 3.3, respectively? State-merging algorithms are one important method that can solve this problem.

---

4. Hence a transcription with stress marked would read LLĤ, LLĤL, and LLĤLH, respectively. It is important not to confuse syllable weight with stress. Here, L and H indicate unstressed "light" and "heavy" syllables, whereas Ĺ and Ĥ will be used to indicate light and heavy syllables bearing primary stress, respectively.

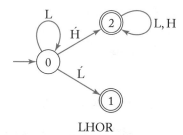

LHOR

FIGURE 3.3: A minimal, deterministic, finite-state acceptor for Kwakwala stress.

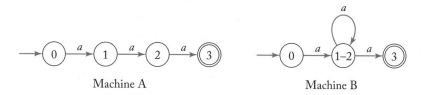

Machine A   Machine B

FIGURE 3.4: Machine B represents the machine obtained by merging states 1 and 2 in Machine A.

3.4.2   MERGING STATES

When distinct states are merged, they become a single state. A key concept in state-merging is that transitions are preserved [Angluin 1982, Hopcroft et al. 2001]. This is one way in which generalizations may occur—because the post-merged machine accepts everything the pre-merged machine accepts, possibly more.

For example in Figure 3.4, Machine B is the machine obtained by merging states 1 and 2 in Machine A. It is necessary to preserve the transitions in Machine A in Machine B. In particular, there must be a transition from state 1 to state 2 in Machine B. There is such a transition, but because states 1 and 2 are the same state in Machine B, the transition is now a loop. Whereas Machine A only accepts one word *aaa*, Machine B accepts an infinite number of words *aa, aaa, aaaa*, ...

Some observations regarding the example in Figure 3.4 are in order. First, the post-merged machine may not be deterministic. Second, the merging process does not specify which states should be merged. It only specifies a mechanism for determining a new machine once it has been decided which states are to be merged. Thus, the choice of which states are to be merged determines the kinds of generalizations that occur. A merging strategy is thus a generalization strategy.

Also, observe that once the equivalence of states is determined, this effectively partitions the states of the acceptor into different regions, or *blocks*. It follows from the definition below that the order in which the states in these regions are merged is inconsequential.

Formally, let $A = \langle \Sigma, Q, I, F, \delta \rangle$ be any NFA. Consider any partition π of Q, and let $B(q, \pi)$ refer to the set of states in the same block of the partition as state q. Then merging states in the same blocks of A according to π yields another acceptor $A/\pi = \langle \Sigma', Q', I', F', \delta' \rangle$ defined as follows:

$$\Sigma' = \Sigma$$

$$Q' = \{B : B(q, \pi) \text{ such that } q \in Q\}$$

$$I' = \{B : B(q, \pi) \text{ such that } q \in I\}$$

$$F' = \{B : B(q, \pi) \text{ such that } q \in F\}$$

$$\delta'(B_0(q_0, \pi), a) = \{B_1(q_1, \pi) : q_1 \in \delta(q_0, a)\}.$$

A/π is sometimes called the *quotient* of A and π. Notice that any block containing at least one final (initial) state is itself a final (initial) state in the new machine. Similarly, if there is at least one transition labeled a from any state in block B_0 to another state in block B_1 then in the new machine there is a transition from B_0 to B_1 labeled a.

The reason state-merging can result in generalization follows from the directly from the following theorem whose origin is unknown. A proof is given in Heinz [2007].

Theorem 3.1   Let A be any acceptor and π any partition of Q. Then $\mathbb{L}(A) \subseteq \mathbb{L}(A/\pi)$.

Thus, according to this theorem, any word accepted by the pre-merged machine will also be accepted by the post-merged machine. The language generated by post-merged machine is necessarily a superset of the pre-merged machine, and this superset language may be infinite in size. Thus, in a very direct way, state-merging shows how it is possible to obtain a grammar which represents a linguistic generalization corresponding to an infinite set from a finite input sample. So this theorem indicates that state-merging is fully capable of modeling such a language learning process. Let us now turn to how the finite input to these algorithms is represented.

3.4.3   FINITE-STATE REPRESENTATIONS OF FINITE SAMPLES

Prefix Trees

A *prefix tree acceptor* (PTA) is a structured, finite-state representation of a finite sample. The idea is that each state in the tree corresponds to a unique prefix in the sample. Here the word "prefix" is not used in its morphological sense, but in its mathematical sense.

Formally, a string u is a *prefix* of a string w iff there exists a string $v \in \Sigma^*$ such that $w = uv$. For every word w, the prefixes of w are $\texttt{prefixes}(w) = \{u \mid u \text{ is a prefix of } w\}$. This function's domain can be extended to languages in the usual way: $\texttt{prefixes}(L) = \bigcup_{w \in L} \texttt{prefixes}(w)$. For every set of strings S, we let $\Sigma(S)$ refer to the alphabet of S.

Now prefix trees can be defined.

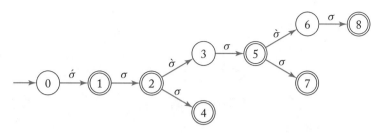

FIGURE 3.5: A prefix tree of Pintupi words.

Definition 3.2   PTA(S) is defined to be the NFA $\langle \Sigma, Q, I, F, \delta \rangle$ such that

$$\Sigma = \Sigma(S)$$
$$Q = \texttt{prefixes}(S)$$
$$I = \{\lambda\}$$
$$F = S$$
$$\delta(u, a) = ua \text{ iff } u, ua \in Q.$$

An example is shown in Figure 3.5, which shows a prefix tree of the syllabic profiles of the eight Pintupi words given in Table 3.2.[5]

Observe that PTA(S) can be computed efficiently in the size of the sample S. PTA(S) can be computed batchwise from a sample S, or iteratively. In the latter case, as each word is added, an existing path in the machine is pursued as far as possible. When no further path exists, a new one is formed. When a word w is added to a prefix tree PTA(S), we speak of *extending* the prefix tree acceptor with w.

Observe further that even in the simple example in Figure 3.5, it is possible to see that there is structure in the prefix tree acceptor, and that this structure repeats itself. State-merging can eliminate this structural redundancy, resulting in generalization.

Suffix Trees

Prefix tree acceptors are not the only way to represent a finite sample as a finite-state machine. Another representation is suffix tree acceptors, which are reverse deterministic representations of the sample.

---

5. We have enumerated the names of the states for convenience. Strictly speaking, according to the definition, state 0 is λ, 1 is $\acute{\sigma}$, 2 is $\acute{\sigma}\sigma$, 3 is $\acute{\sigma}\sigma\grave{\sigma}$, and so on.

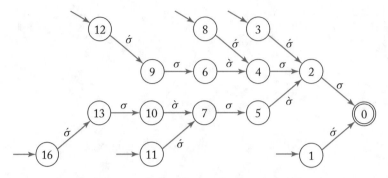

FIGURE 3.6: A suffix tree for Pintupi words.

Formally, a string u is a *suffix* of a string w if_{def} there exists a string $v \in \Sigma^*$ such that $w = vu$. The suffixes of words and languages are defined analogously as above and is denoted with suffixes($\cdot$).

Definition 3.3   STA(S) is defined to be the acceptor $\langle \Sigma, Q, I, F, \delta \rangle$ such that

$$\Sigma = \Sigma(S)$$
$$Q = \texttt{suffixes}(S)$$
$$I = S$$
$$F = \{\lambda\}$$
$$\delta(au, a) = u \text{ iff } u, ua \in Q.$$

As an example, Figure 3.6 shows a suffix tree for the same eight Pintupi words.

Like prefix trees, suffix trees can also be constructed efficiently with batch or iterative algorithms.

3.4.4   THE STATE-MERGING THEOREM

It has been proved that if a sample of words generated by some NFA is sufficient—that is, exercises every transition in this NFA—then there exists some way to merge states in the prefix tree to recover the generating NFA [Angluin 1982]. Although we do not know which states should be merged, we are guaranteed that there is a way to merge such states to recover the original machine. We know such a partition exists.

The theorem is given below after some helpful definitions.

Definition 3.4   Let $A = \langle \Sigma, Q, q_0, F, \delta \rangle$ be a tail canonical acceptor, and let $w \in \mathbb{L}(A)$. Then the *transition set* of w are those transitions in δ that make up the path of w through A (recall that for each $w \in \mathbb{L}(A)$, there is a unique path since A is tail canonical). We denote the transition set of w in A with $\mathtt{Trans\_set}_A(w)$.

Definition 3.5   Let $A = \langle \Sigma, Q, q_0, F, \delta \rangle$ be a canonical finite-state acceptor. Then S is a sufficient sample of A if_{def} $\bigcup_{w \in S} \mathtt{Trans\_set}_A(w) = \delta$ and for all $q_f \in F$, there is a word $w \in S$ such that $\delta(q_0, w) = q_f$.

Pictorially, we can imagine, as A computes the path of some word w, coloring the states and transitions along this path. If a sample S is sufficient for a canonical acceptor then every state and transition will be colored after every word in S is processed. Additionally, we can imagine marking final states when we reach the end of the string. Importantly, since Q is finite, there will be sufficient samples that only contain *finitely* many strings.[6]

Theorem 3.2   Let $A = \langle \Sigma, Q, I, F, \delta \rangle$ be a tail canonical finite-state acceptor, S a finite sufficient sample of A, and $\mathrm{PTA}(S) = \langle \Sigma_{PT}, Q_{PT}, I_{PT}, F_{PT}, \delta_{PT} \rangle$. Then there exists a partition π over Q_{PT} such that $\mathrm{PTA}(S)/\pi$ is isomorphic to A.

A corollary follows that state-merging over suffix trees is also viable.

Corollary 3.1   Let $A = \langle \Sigma, Q, I, F, \delta \rangle$ be a head canonical finite-state acceptor, S a finite sufficient sample of A, and $\mathrm{STA}(S) = \langle \Sigma_{ST}, Q_{ST}, I_{ST}, F_{ST}, \delta_{ST} \rangle$. Then there exists a partition π over Q_{ST} such that $\mathrm{STA}(S)/\pi$ is isomorphic to A.

A proof of the theorem and its corollary can be found in Heinz [2007].

The significance of this theorem (and corollary) should not be overlooked. Provided the learning data D exercises every transition in the target finite-state grammar, there is a way to merge states in the prefix tree built from D which exactly yields the learning target. Since there are only finitely many transitions, only a finite sample is needed to meet this condition. Thus, the possibility is raised that—for some subclass of the regular languages—there is a state-merging strategy which identifies that class in the limit from positive data.

State-merging algorithms therefore can be stated very simply. Given a finite sample S, a state-merging algorithm first computes either the prefix or suffix tree of S, and then computes a partition π of this tree and finally computes the quotient of this tree according to the partition π. In other words, the algorithm returns a machine M equal to the following:

$$M = T(S)/\pi, \tag{3.1}$$

---

6. Typically, a shortest transition set can be constructed as follows. For each state q, take the shortest string w that reaches q from the initial state. Then, to this set add wa for each $a \in \Sigma$.

where $T(S)$ is either a prefix or suffix tree acceptor. In this way, state-merging algorithms are able to determine the *global* structure of the final DFA through a series of *local* decisions in the prefix tree. This is possible because the canonical form of the DFA provides a sound rationale for such local decisions to be made. States are merged if there is reason to believe that distinct prefixes have the same set of tails, according to the Myhill–Nerode relation.

The problem of learning stress patterns can now be restated in this context. How can states be merged in the prefix tree for Pintupi (Figure 3.5) to return an acceptor equivalent to the one in Figure 3.2? Will the same merging strategy yield the stress pattern of Kwakwala (Figure 3.3) when given a prefix tree acceptor for Kwakwala words?

3.5   STATE-MERGING AS A LEARNING BIAS

Theorem 3.2 establishes a key result: Given any tail canonical acceptor A for any regular language and a sufficient sample S of words generated by this acceptor, there is some way to merge states in the prefix tree of S which returns the acceptor A. This result does not tell us which states to merge for a particular acceptor. It just says that there is partition of states whose blocks, once merged, would yield an acceptor isomorphic to the canonical one. Nonetheless, the result is important because it leaves open the possibility that there is some property of a class of regular sets we may be interested in for which there is a successful state-merging strategy.

This section reviews state-merging strategies that have been employed for learning regular sets and regular relations and the kinds of regular sets and relations that are learnable by those strategies.

One strategy for merging states examines structural properties of the tree acceptors. For example, two states may be deemed equivalent if they share the same incoming paths of length 2. Formally, this means states in the prefix tree $\text{PTA}(S) = \langle \Sigma, Q, I, F, \delta \rangle$ are merged if they have the same k-length suffix. For all $u, v \in Q$:

$$u \sim v \; \text{if}_{def} \; \exists x, y, w \text{ such that } |w| = k, u = xw, v = yw. \tag{3.2}$$

This state-merging algorithm then is simply the one shown in Equation 3.3:

$$G = \text{PTA}(S)/\pi_{\sim}. \tag{3.3}$$

To illustrate the algorithm, consider the prefix tree for Pintupi words (Figure 3.5). It is easily seen that states 4 and 7 share the same incoming path ($\sigma\sigma$). States 3 and 6 share $\grave{\sigma}\sigma$, and 5 and 8 share $\sigma\grave{\sigma}$. Merging these states yields the Figure 3.7. The acceptor in Figure 3.7 is not the canonical acceptor for Pintupi, but it does recognize the same language.

In fact, this algorithm provably identifies in the limit from positive data the Strictly $(k + 1)$-Local class of languages [García and Vidal 1990]. Strictly k-Local languages are a subregular class

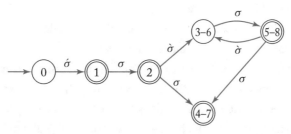

FIGURE 3.7: The result of merging states in the prefix tree for Pintupi words (Figure 3.5) with the same incoming paths of length 2.

of formal languages which are the non-stochastic counterparts to n-gram models (where $n = k + 1$). They have been studied extensively [McNaughton and Papert 1971, Rogers and Pullum 2011, Rogers et al. 2013].

Edlefsen et al. [2008] study whether 109 distinct stress patterns are Strictly k-Local and if so for what k. These 109 patterns are taken from typological studies [Bailey 1995, Gordon 2002] and have been encoded as NFA [Heinz 2009].[7] They find that only 44 of these patterns are Strictly 2-Local and 81 are Strictly 5-Local. They find that the other 28 are not Strictly k-Local for any k. In other words, even permitting very generous input samples, only 81 of the patterns can be learned by merging states with the same incoming paths of length 5, and 28 cannot be learned by merging states with the same incoming paths of length k, for any k. Is there a state-merging strategy that works for *all* 109 distinct stress patterns?

There are other ways to merge states. Generally, two strategies are followed. First, if the current structure is "ill-formed" then merge states to eliminate sources of ill-formedness. The state-merging strategy described above is an example of this approach. A prefix tree with multiple states with the same incoming path of length k is "ill-formed" and this "defect" is corrected by merging these states. Angluin [1982] recursively merged states to eliminate reverse non-determinism and proves that this procedure identifies the 0-reversible languages (and generalizes the procedure to learn the class of reversible languages). Muggleton [1990] merged states with the same "contexts" of size k and proves the learnability of the k-contextual languages. Heinz [2008] merged final states and proves this procedure learns the class of left-to-right iterative languages, which are classes related to the zero-reversible class. This kind of state-merging has also been studied in the context learning stochastic regular languages. For example, Stolcke [1994] merged states to maximize posterior probability (for

---

7. These NFA are available at http://st2.ullet.net.

HMMs), and Carrasco and Oncina [1999] merged states in a prefix tree if the residual stochastic language of each prefix with respect to the tree are sufficiently similar.

The second merging strategy is to enumerate the states in the prefix tree and begin to merge states in that order unless "ill-formed" structures arise. For instance, RPNI merges states unless the resulting generalization is inconsistent with the negative data (the finite sample to RPNI includes both positive and negative examples). Similarly, Oncina et al. [1993] proved the learnability of subsequential transducers by merging states unless "onward subsequentiality" is lost. Clark and Thollard [2004] presented a learnability result for regular stochastic languages by merging states unless they are "μ-distinguishable." These algorithms are discussed in further detail below.

To summarize, state-merging strategies instantiate learning biases. This is because distinctions maintained in the prefix tree (or suffix tree) are lost by state-merging, which results in generalizations. The choice of partition corresponds to the generalization strategy (i.e., which distinctions will be maintained and which will be lost). As Gleitman [1990, p. 12] wrote:

> The trouble is that an observer who notices *everything* can learn *nothing* for there is no end of categories known and constructible to describe a situation. [emphasis in original]

The prefix tree keeps track of all the information, and state-merging deliberately ignores some of it, leading to generalization. Which information should be ignored and which should be kept is at the heart of learning, and at the heart of state-merging.

3.6   STATE-MERGING AS INFERENCE RULES

One of the important insights that state-merging learning strategies has led to is the relationship of the Nerode-equivalence relation to other kinds of equivalence relations. Two examples will serve to illustrate.

Again consider the strictly k-local languages [McNaughton and Papert 1971, García et al. 1990], which can be learned by merging states with same incoming paths of length k. Because these states are merged it means any two prefixes of the languages with the same k-length suffix have exactly the same residuals; that is, they have the same set of good tails. Formally, this can be stated as an inference rule: $\forall u, v, w \in \Sigma^* : uv, wv \in \texttt{prefixes}(L)$ with $|v| = k$ then $\texttt{Tails}_L(uv) = \texttt{Tails}_L(wv)$. This property turns out to be a characteristic property of the strictly local languages known as the *suffix substitution property* [Rogers and Pullum 2011]: a language L is Strictly Local $if_{def} \exists k$ such that if $uvx, wvy \in L$ and $|v| = k$ then $uvy, wvx \in L$. The state-merging makes clear why this property holds—paths uv and wv will lead to the same state.

Another example comes from the 0-reversible languages [Angluin 1982]. Angluin showed that by merging states to eliminate reverse non-determinism that $\forall u, v, w, y \in \Sigma^*$ if $uv, wv, uy \in L$ then $wy \in L$. In other words, if two prefixes u and w share one good tail then they share all good tails.

The insights by understanding these state-merging algorithms in terms of inference rules of the above types have led to a number of algorithms for learning non-regular languages under the name "distributional learning" [Clark and Eyraud 2007, Yoshinaka 2009, Clark and Lappin 2011].

3.7   RPNI

RPNI is an acronym for Regular Positive and Negative Inference. As its name indicates, RPNI is unlike the state-merging algorithms considered so far because it relies on both positive and negative evidence. A detailed discussion (with theorems and proofs) along with a clear explanation of an example run of RPNI is provided by de la Higuera [2010]. The brief discussion draws highlights from de la Higuera's discussion there.

3.7.1   HOW IT WORKS

Like the state-merging algorithms above, RPNI first builds a prefix tree from the positive data. Note that the negative data is not expressed in the prefix tree. There is only one way in which it could in fact be expressed. If a negative data point w was a prefix of a positive data point wv, then the state in the prefix tree corresponding to w could be marked as "definitively not a final state." This foretells how the merging procedure in RPNI uses the negative evidence.

After the prefix tree is built, the states are enumerated in a breadth-first fashion. Figure 3.8 illustrates a breadth-first enumeration of a prefix tree. Pairs of states are merged (and then tested) according to this enumeration. So in Figure 3.8, RPNI first merges states 0 and 1 and tests the consequences (see below). This test determines whether those states should stay merged or if the merge should be undone. Afterwards, in either case, it considers the next pair of states in the enumeration. In this example, that would be states 0 and 2, then 0 and 3, then 1 and 2, and so on.

One consequence of this particular enumeration is that whenever two states are merged, one of those states will always be the root of a subtree. In other words, the tails of one of the two states being merged in the prefix tree will always be finite.[8]

The automata obtained from merging of two states is then tested against the negative evidence. If this automata rejects all the available negative evidence then the test is a success; otherwise it fails. If the test fails, merging of the two states is undone, and the two states remain distinct henceforth.

To see why the test could fail, recall that if a final state is merged with a non-final state, the resulting state is also final. If this non-final state is one that *must* be non-final given the negative evidence, then the test will fail. For instance, if trying to learn a regular language L, the positive examples in Figure 3.8 are provided, and it is known that $a \notin L$, then merging states 1 and 2 will

---

8. In de la Higuera's book, these are referred to as the "blue" states.

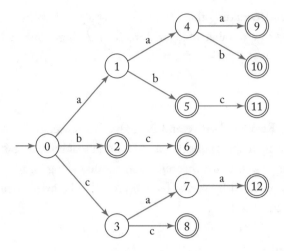

FIGURE 3.8: A prefix-tree whose states have been enumerated in breadth-first fashion.

be rejected. This is because the merged state will be final which would result in an automata which misclassifies the string a. This is how RPNI uses negative evidence.

Another important detail regarding RPNI is how it handles non-determinism. Recall that state-merging can (and often does) lead to non-determinism. Essentially, once a pair of states has been merged, the non-determinism is eliminated by "folding" the tree branching from one of the merged states into the rest of the existing automata, extending it as necessary. Thus, if a merge is rejected, the folding must also be undone.

3.7.2   THEORETICAL RESULTS

Oncina et al. [1993] proved that the RPNI efficiently identifies all regular languages in the limit from positive and negative data. The proof establishes the existence of a (finite) characteristic sample for each regular language. This characteristic sample can be determined from the tail canonical acceptor. Essentially, the positive data comes from a finite set of words which exercise every transition (and final states) in the automata. The crucial negative evidence comes from data points which show that every two states in the canonical acceptor do not have the same set of tails. Since both the positive and negative evidence are finite, the entire sample itself is finite as well.

As an example, consider the canonical acceptor for Pintupi stress. A negative data point which distinguishes states 2 and 3 would be $\acute{\sigma}\sigma\sigma\grave{\sigma}\sigma$ since $\grave{\sigma}\sigma$ is a tail of $\acute{\sigma}\sigma$ (which leads to state 2), but it is not a tail of $\acute{\sigma}\sigma\sigma$ (which leads to state 3).

One important aspect of RPNI is that it is an efficient algorithm in a couple of different senses. First, its execution time is polynomial in the size of the sample. Second, and more interestingly, the size of the characteristic sample is polynomial in the size of the canonical acceptor for the target regular language.

It is the second property which distinguishes RPNI from learners mentioned in Chapter 2. Recall in Section 2.2.2 that there are learning algorithms that are able to learn the entire computably enumerable class from positive and negative data. These algorithms enumerated all the logically possibly grammars and just hypothesized the first one in the enumeration consistent with all the data considered so far. These "enumerative learners" were troubling because while they met the letter of the definition of learning, they did not meet its spirit. They were not insightful, and suggested something about the definition was not correct.

One way to improve the definition was to require learning to be efficient in some sense. Of the two senses mentioned above, with respect to regular languages—polynomial-time computability in the size of the data and polynomial size of the characteristic sample in the size of the canonical acceptor for target language—only the latter is meaningful. This is because Pitt [1989] showed that any enumerative learner can be made polynomial-time computable in the size of the data with a method now referred to as Pitt's trick. (See also de la Higuera [1997, 2010], Eyraud et al. [2015].)

No such trick is known to exist for the second sense, which is "polynomial size of the characteristic sample in the size of the canonical acceptor." Thus, it is this second sense which makes RPNI an interesting contribution to the problem of inference of regular languages from positive and negative data.

3.8   REGULAR RELATIONS

Regular relations are those relations that can be described with non-deterministic finite-state transducers. Many problems in computational linguistics, such as transliteration, letter-to-phoneme conversion, and machine translation, are problems about learning relations.

Subsequential relations are a subclass of the regular relations. They are those regular relations which describe *functions* for which a finite-state transducer which processes the input deterministically exists. They can also be described informally as weighted deterministic acceptors where the weights are strings and multiplication is concatenation.

Formally, a *subsequential* transducer is a tuple $\langle Q, q_0, X, Y, \sigma, \delta \rangle$, where Q is a finite set of states, X and Y are finite alphabets, $q_0 \in Q$ is the initial state, and $\sigma \subseteq Q \times Y^*$ is the output function. The transition function $\delta \subseteq Q \times X \times Y^* \times Q$ is necessarily deterministic:

$$(q, a, u, r), (q, a, v, s) \in \delta \Rightarrow u = v \wedge r = s.$$

The transition function δ is also recursively extended to δ^*. The relation that a subsequential transducer $T = \langle Q, q_0, X, Y, \sigma, \delta \rangle$ recognizes/accepts/generates is

$$R(t) = \Big\{ (x, yz) \in X^* \times Y^* \mid (\exists q \in F)$$

$$[(q_0, x, y, q) \in \delta^* \wedge z = \sigma(q)]\Big\}. \tag{3.4}$$

Since subsequential transducers are deterministic, the relations they recognize are functions. Subsequential transducers have been generalized to permit up to p outputs for each input and Mohri [1997] showed that many desirable properties are preserved.

Like NFA, subsequential transducers have a canonical form [Oncina et al. 1993], which associates the states of the canonical machine to classes of a Nerode-like equivalence. In addition to the aforementioned properties of subsequential transducers, these canonical machines are "onward," which means the transducer, as it reads the input, minimally delays writing the output (so not at all or as little as possible).

Oncina et al. [1993] presented the Onward Subsequential Transducer Inference Algorithm (OSTIA), which provably identifies subsequential functions in the limit from positive data. For every subsequential function f, the input to the algorithm is a finite sample of pairs $(w, f(w))$. OSTIA is similar to RPNI because pairs $(w, f(w))$ provide a form of (indirect) negative evidence. If $(x, y) \in f$ then for all $z \neq y$ it must be the case that $(x, z) \notin f$.

OSTIA first builds an onward prefix tree. An onward prefix tree is constructed based on the input strings and the outputs are pushed as close to the root of the tree as possible to ensure onwardness. Then the algorithm merges states in a manner similar to RPNI. It enumerates the states in the prefix tree in a breadth-first fashion and then greedily merges states unless onward subsequentiality is lost.

Oncina et al. [1993] proved that OSTIA identifies total subsequential functions in the limit from positive data. Again, no negative data is required (unlike RPNI) because the positive data, in conjunction with the knowledge that a function is being learned, provides *indirect* negative evidence.

Interestingly, for partial subsequential functions f, OSTIA is also guaranteed to succeed in the sense that it returns a subsequential function f' such that for all w in the domain of f it is the case that $f'(w) = f(w)$. But, interestingly, if f is not defined on w, f' may be! Oncina et al. [1993] reported an interesting experiment on learning the function converting Roman numerals to Arabic numerals, where the function returned by OSTIA correctly translates well-defined Roman numerals like "XVIII" but returns uninterpretable numbers on ill-defined Roman numerals like "VXIII."

Also, in later work Oncina and colleagues overcome this challenge by changing the nature of the learning problem. If the learning problem is to identify a subsequential transduction given a learning sample *and the domain* of the transduction (given as a DFA) then they showed even partial subsequential transduction can be efficiently identified exactly [Oncina and Varó 1996]. Similarly, they show how additional knowledge of the range helps in a similar way [Castellanos et al. 1998].

OSTIA has also been applied to phonological rule learning. Gildea and Jurafsky [1996] show that OSTIA does not learn the English tapping rule or German word-final devoicing rule from data present in adapted dictionaries of English or German. They explain that the sufficient sample that OSTIA needs to converge (and is guaranteed to receive as input at some finite point in theory under the identification in the limit from positive data paradigm) is not present in these adapted dictionaries. This is not just a matter of quantity and needing larger dictionaries. It is also a matter of quality. The sufficient sample needed by OSTIA to learn these phonological rules may require words that violate inviolable constraints in English and German, such as the logically possible word *ttt*. Gildea and Jurafsky [1996] went on to apply additional phonologically-motivated heuristics to improve state-merging choices and obtain significantly better results.

More recently, Chandlee [2014] shows local phonological processes can be characterized by a class of subsequential functions. This subclass is called *input strictly local* because they are defined analogously to the strictly local languages. Chandlee et al. [2014] provides a state-merging algorithm which learns this subclass in the limit from positive data more efficiently than OSTIA or its variants. Jardine et al. [2014] provides another algorithm for learning this subclass from positive examples in linear time and data as well as other subclasses whose underlying structure is known and fixed in advance. These algorithms are similar in flavor to the variants of OSTIA which also assume additional a priori knowledge [Oncina and Varó 1996, Castellanos et al. 1998] (but in terms of the nature of the transduction in addition to knowledge of the domain or range).

3.9   LEARNING STOCHASTIC REGULAR LANGUAGES

In this section, the grammatical inference of regular stochastic languages is examined. After defining regular stochastic languages, the first problem is considered: how to estimate the parameters, from a sample, of a stochastic language belonging to a class of subregular distributions describable with a deterministic finite-state acceptor (PFA). This problem has a known solution under the Maximum Likelihood Estimate criteria. After discussing two classes of subregular stochastic distributions, we move to state-merging algorithms which are able to efficiently learn the entire class of regular deterministic stochastic languages under different learning criteria. Methods that target the larger class of regular *non*-deterministic stochastic languages are then discussed. This discussion includes mention of the results of the recent PAUTOMAC competition, where teams competed to develop algorithms that could best learn deterministic and non-deterministic regular stochastic languages [Verwer et al. 2014].

3.9.1   STOCHASTIC LANGUAGES

A stochastic language is a probability distribution over Σ^*. As explained in Chapter 2, this means that

1. each word in Σ^* is assigned some probability between zero and one, and

2. the sum of all the probabilities adds to one.

Like formal (non-stochastic) languages, there are different classes of stochastic languages. As with non-stochastic languages, the field of grammatical inference is interested in finding algorithms that can successfully learn every distribution in a class, under some rigorous definition of successful learning.

One way to define classes of stochastic languages is in terms of the *support* of the stochastic languages. The support of a stochastic language is the non-stochastic language obtained by the set of strings with non-zero probabilities. While it is natural to define regular stochastic languages as those with regular support (and context-free stochastic languages as those with context-free support and so on), these are not very useful definitions. For instance, if regular stochastic languages are defined as those with regular support then very powerful grammars are necessary to compute them [Kornai 2011]. This result, originally due to Ellis [1969], is because there are logically possible distributions with regular support where the probabilities contain irrational values. In fact, Kornai (Theorem 1) actually shows that even probabilistic context-free grammars cannot describe all stochastic languages with regular support. Consequently, the distinctions afforded by the traditional class boundaries—regular, context-free, context-sensitive, and computably enumerable—are lost. For this reason we define classes of stochastic languages in terms of the grammars, and not in terms of their support.

It is common in computational linguistics for stochastic grammars of a certain type to be defined as their non-stochastic counterparts. For instance, a probabilistic context-free grammar is simply a context-free grammar where the production rules have been augmented with probabilities in an appropriate fashion. Similarly, regular stochastic languages can be defined to be those describable with finite-state machines augmented with probabilities on the transitions. (This class turns out to be exactly the same class of distributions that can be represented with hidden Markov models [Vidal et al. 2005]; see Chapter 2). When classes of stochastic languages are defined in this way, the traditional boundaries remain [Kornai 2011, Theorem 2]. For example, with these definitions, any distribution defined by a stochastic NFA can be defined by a PCFG, but not vice versa. It is this (grammar-based) definition that we use when discussing families of stochastic languages.

As with classes of formal languages, even if two classes are learnable under some definition of learning, there is typically a trade-off in the amount of time and data necessary to converge to the target grammar depending on the nature of the target class. The more structured the class (and hence typically less expressive), the easier learning tends to be.

As mentioned, regular distributions are those obtained by assigning probabilities to the transitions of each state in a (possibly non-deterministic) finite-state acceptor.[9] Consequently, there are two problems when trying to learn a regular distribution: one is trying to learn the structure of the finite-state acceptor, and one is trying to learn the probabilities on the transitions. By structure of the acceptor, we mean the state set and the transitions between the states. Since any missing transition can be modeled as an existing transition with zero probability, the structure of every acceptor can be considered to be fully connected (every transition with every letter of the alphabet exists between every two states). This effectively reduces the structure of the machines to a single number—the number of states in the acceptor.

Learning the class of regular distributions is not easy, but there has been substantial theoretical progress in grammatical inference which addresses this problem. We begin this section with a much easier problem: learning very structured classes of distributions using the Maximum Likelihood Estimate as the learning criterion.

Many readers are probably familiar with this style of learning since it underlies commonly used techniques in natural language processing (such as n-grams). An orthodox presentation can be found in many places, such as Geman and Johnson [2004].

However, the presentation here is unorthodox because it is being presented from the perspective of grammatical inference. Our focus is on well-defined classes of distributions, well-defined presentations of data drawn from these distributions, well-defined learning criteria that make clear what successful learning is, and algorithms that successfully learn any distribution from the class under this learning criteria.

3.9.2   STRUCTURE OF THE CLASS IS DETERMINISTIC AND KNOWN A PRIORI

One way a class of stochastic distributions can be described is with a *single* deterministic finite-state acceptor. The DFA represents a class of distributions—the ones obtainable by placing probabilities on the transitions in the DFA. In order to keep the grammatical representation finite, it will be important to constrain the probabilities on the transitions in some fashion. It is common to assume they have rational values and cannot be any real value. We will abstract away from this issue here.

Clearly, this class is properly contained within the class of regular distributions. For a DFA $\mathcal{M}$, let $\mathfrak{D}_{\mathcal{M}}$ denote this class of distributions. This class essentially fixes the structure, and thus the only learning problem is to learn probabilities of the transitions. Figure 3.9 illustrates a class of distributions and a particular distribution within the class.

---

9. Here, and in the sequel, we consider the action of ending the generation process at a particular state with a transitional probability. Formally, this is usually accomplished with a function which maps states (not transitions) to probability.

FIGURE 3.9: $\mathcal{M}$ represents a family of distributions with four parameters. $\mathcal{M}'$ represents a particular distribution in this family.

The statistical model is given by the structure of the DFA and the transitions to be estimated are the parameters of the model. This problem has a solution under the learning criterion known as the Maximum Likelihood Estimate (MLE).

To explain the MLE criterion, it is necessary to first define the likelihood of a sample S generated by a distribution $\mathcal{D}$. Let $\mathcal{D}(w)$ be the probability that $\mathcal{D}$ generates w. If $S = \langle w_1, \ldots w_n \rangle$ then the likelihood of S given $\mathcal{D}$ is defined as

$$L_{\mathcal{D}}(S) = \prod_{w \in S} \mathcal{D}(w).$$

Note that S is not a set, but a sequence, so the same word can occur multiple times in S (and thus would occur multiple times in the product). The product above reflects the assumption that S is independent and identically distributed (i.i.d.). Therefore, an element in the sequence S is independent of the ones that come before and after it.

Given a sample of data S, the MLE of S is the distribution $\mathcal{D}_A \in \mathcal{D}$ that maximizes the likelihood of the data S with respect to the $\mathcal{D}$. In other words, MLE assigns a greater likelihood to S than every other distribution in $\mathcal{D}$.

The MLE learning criterion can then be stated as follows. A learning algorithm $\mathcal{A}$ learns a class of distributions $\mathcal{D}$ if_{def}, for all $\mathcal{D}$ belonging to $\mathcal{D}$, and for any finite sample of data S generated by $\mathcal{D}$, the grammar G output by $\mathcal{A}(S)$ defines a distribution $\mathcal{D}_G$, which is the MLE with respect to $\mathcal{D}$.

One of the reasons the MLE criterion is important follows from thinking of the input sample S as it becomes longer and longer and approaches an *infinite* sequence of words generated by the target distribution. For any $\epsilon > 0$, there is a sample size N such that for all S where $|S| \geq N$, the difference between the MLE of S with respect to $\mathcal{D}$ and the true distribution $\mathcal{D} \in \mathcal{D}$ is within ϵ. This property is called *consistency* in the statistical literature. In other words, we are guaranteed, as

FIGURE 3.10: The figure on the left indicates the count of the parse of $S = \langle bbc \rangle$ through $\mathcal{M}$ and the figure on the right indicates the probabilities obtained after normalization.

the sample size grows, to get arbitrarily close to the true distribution. The difference between two distributions can be measured in different ways, but the above result is true for any of these ways.[10]

For any DFA $\mathcal{M}$, a learning algorithm for $\mathfrak{D}_{\mathcal{M}}$ which satisfies the MLE is known. We do not know the origins of the following theorem, but it is not difficult to prove.[11] For modern treatments, see Vidal et al. [2005] and de la Higuera [2010].

Theorem 3.3 For a sample S and deterministic finite-state acceptor $\mathcal{M}$, let algorithm $\mathcal{A}$ count the parse of S through $\mathcal{M}$ and normalize at each state. $\mathcal{A}$ is a learning algorithm for $\mathfrak{D}_{\mathcal{M}}$ which satisfies the MLE.

To count the parse of S through $\mathcal{M}$ means the following. Initialize the count of each transition, and the count of ending at each state to zero. Then, for each word $w \in S$, follow the path of w in $\mathcal{M}$ and add one to each transition traversed in this path. When a word ends in a state, add one to that count as well. Since w was generated by a distribution in $\mathfrak{D}_{\mathcal{M}}$ and since $\mathcal{M}$ is deterministic, there is exactly one such path. In the statistical literature, this kind of learning process is called the *relative frequency estimator*.

Figure 3.10 illustrates the learning procedure of $\mathfrak{D}_{\mathcal{M}}$ for $S = \langle bbc \rangle$. According to Theorem 3.3, the PFA on the right in Figure 3.10 satisfies the MLE criterion: the likelihood it assigns to $S = \langle bbc \rangle$ is greater than the likelihood every other distribution in $\mathfrak{D}_{\mathcal{M}}$ assigns to S.

N-gram models are widely used in computational linguistics. These are in fact strictly k-local distributions. Figure 3.11 shows the structure of a bi-gram model where the alphabet is $\{a, b, c\}$. Such a model has 16 transitional probabilities, given by associating probabilities to each transition and to ending at each state. These are the 16 parameters of a bi-gram model for this alphabet.

---

10. de la Higuera [2010] and Clark and Lappin [2011] contain good discussions of different ways measures to measure the distance between distributions.

11. A typical proof of this theorem solves a system of partial differential equations.

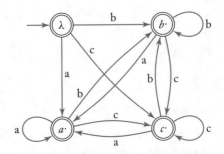

FIGURE 3.11: The structure of a bi-gram model.

TABLE 3.4: Words in Samala with sibilant sounds [ʃ, S]

1.	[ʃtojonowonowaʃ]	"it stood upright"	[Applegate 1972, p. 72]
2.	[kʃipïtwaʃ]	"I made acorn mush"	[Applegate 1972, p. 119]
3.	[suslasïq]	"he presses it tight"	[Applegate 1972, p. 119]
4.	[swasʰisin]	"the terrain is rugged"	[Applegate 1972, p. 122]

Leaving aside the important problem of smoothing [Jurafsky and Martin 2008, Ch. 4], training a bi-gram model proceeds exactly per Theorem 3.3.

It is well known that natural language contains long-distance dependencies, both in syntax [Chomsky 1956] and in phonology [Odden 1994, Rose and Walker 2004, Hansson 2010, Nevins 2010]. For any n, these dependencies can extend beyond n symbols, and so n-gram models are unable to express (or model) them.

Here is an example of an unbounded long-distance dependency from Samala,[12] a Chumash language spoken in an area near Santa Barbara, California [Applegate 1972, 2007]. In this language, there is a long-distance dependency among sibilant sounds. Sibilants are sounds like [ʃ, s], and in Samala there are words containing sounds like [ʃ] and words containing sounds like [s], but no words containing both [ʃ, s]. Well-formed words only draw from one group of these sounds or the other and never from both. Some Samala words are shown in Table 3.4. However, there are no words which are normally pronounced like those shown in Table 3.5.

This kind of long-distance dependency can be modeled with strictly piecewise languages [Heinz 2010, Rogers et al. 2010, 2013]. These are a subclass of the regular languages similar to strictly

---

12. This language was formerly called Ineseño Chumash.

TABLE 3.5: Impossible Samala words with sibilant sounds [s, ʃ]

1.	*[stojonowonowaʃ]
2.	*[ʃtojonowonowas]
3.	*[koswasʰiʃin]
4.	*[koʃwasʰisin]

local languages, except they are based on *subsequences*, not *substrings*. A word u is a subsequence of another word w the symbols in u occur in the same order in w (but not necessarily contiguously).[13] With respect to Samala, this means that words like *[stojonowonowaʃ] and *[ʃtojonowonowas] are ill-formed because the *subsequences* **sʃ** and **ʃs**, which these words contain, are ill-formed.[14]

The strictly piecewise languages have several interesting characterizations in terms of formal language theory, automata theory, model theory [Rogers et al. 2010, 2013], and the algebraic theory of automata [Fu et al. 2011]. Like strictly local languages, if there is an upper bound k on the length of the sequence, the class is also provably efficiently learnable in interesting ways [Heinz et al. 2012b, Heinz and Rogers 2013].

Heinz and Rogers [2010] defined strictly piecewise distributions and present an algorithm for learning the MLE of this class. They represent the class with multiple machines (what Heinz and Rogers [2013] call a "factored" representation). The distribution itself is then provided by a variant of the product operation which calculates the co-emission probability [Vidal et al. 2005]. The algorithm finds the MLE of the class of distributions represented by each individual factor per Theorem 3.3, and then applies the product operation.

The results in Table 3.6 show the parameters obtained when the algorithm is fed a training corpus of 4800 words from a dictionary of Samala. The results mean *[stojonowonowaʃ] would be orders of magnitude less likely than [ʃtojonowonowaʃ] because it contains the [sʃ] subsequence.

This example, and the one before it, are examples of subregular classes of distributions, which can be represented with a single automaton as in the case of the strictly k-local languages, or as a list of automata which are combined by a special product operation, as in the case of the strictly k-piecewise languages. What they have in common is that the structure of the class can be fixed to these automata-theoretic representations. Consequently, learning distributions based on these

---

13. Formal definitions are given in Section 1.6. The language $\Sigma^* u_1 \Sigma^* u_2 \cdots \Sigma^* u_n \Sigma^*$ is called the *shuffle ideal* of u.

14. There are languages like Samala except only one of the subsequences {**sʃ**, **ʃs**} is forbidden. See Heinz [2010] for discussion.

TABLE 3.6: SP_2 probabilities of a sibilant occurring some-time after another one (collapsing laryngeal distinctions). $P(x \mid y <)$ means the probability of x given y occuring anywhere before it in the string.

$P(x \mid y <)$		x			
		s	$\widehat{ts}$	ʃ	tʃ
y	s	0.0325	0.0051	0.0013	0.0002
	$\widehat{ts}$	0.0212	0.0114	0.0008	0.
	ʃ	0.0011	0.	0.067	0.0359
	$\widehat{tʃ}$	0.0006	0.	0.0458	0.0314

classes can be reduced to the problem of the estimating the values of the parameters of the model, which are expressed in the automata as the transitional probabilities. Theorem 3.3 is an important result allowing this to happen.

This section has focused on learning stochastic languages where the underlying structure is fixed with a single DFA (as is the case for stochastic strictly k-local languages, also called n-gram models), or is fixed with a list of DFA (as is the case for stochastic strictly k-piecewise languages) under the MLE learning criterion. Other types of learning criteria, and other types of estimators exist, which can also be profitably studied when the structure of the is known and fixed a priori. Chapter 2 already discussed the PAC-learning criteria. Bayes estimators and the *maximum a posteriori* estimator are also widely used in computational linguistics and natural language processing [Geman and Johnson 2004].

So far this chapter has motivated the strictly local and strictly piecewise languages from studies of natural language phonotactics. More generally, it has been hypothesized that all segmental phonotactic patterns in natural languages can be modeled with strictly local and strictly piecewise languages (and by extension, distributions) [Heinz 2010]. (See Heinz et al. [2011] for a slightly weaker hypothesis.)

3.9.3   STRUCTURE OF THE CLASS IS DETERMINISTIC BUT NOT KNOWN A PRIORI

There are algorithms with theoretical guarantees for larger classes of regular distributions. In particular, the class of regular deterministic stochastic languages is identifiable in the limit with probability one [de la Higuera and Thollard 2000] and are learnable in modified-PAC setting [Clark and Thollard 2004].

In both cases, the algorithms presented employ state-merging methods and build on prior work, notably the algorithm ALERGIA [Carrasco and Oncina 1994], which is the first approach guaranteed to learn the structure underlying *any* regular deterministic stochastic language (RDSL). In this section, we choose to describe ALERGIA [Carrasco and Oncina 1994, 1999], because of its similarity to RPNI and OSTIA.

For non-stochastic regular languages, we already emphasized the importance of the Myhill–Nerode theorem. A similar theorem exists for regular deterministic stochastic languages [Carrasco and Oncina 1999, Vidal et al. 2005]. Each RDSL has a canonical representation in terms of a probabilistic deterministic finite-state acceptor (DPFA). Just as each state q in the tail canonical acceptor for a regular language corresponds to a regular language, which is the set of good tails for each string w that leads to q from the initial state, each state in the canonical DPFA for a RDSL corresponds to a RDSL, which represents the residual for each string w that leads to q from the initial state with a non-zero probability. In this case, the residual is a *stochastic* language.

Consequently, a state-merging algorithm needs only to decide correctly whether two states in a prefix tree construction have the same stochastic set of good tails. The general form of the algorithm is given by RLIPS [Carrasco and Oncina 1994], which is an acronym for Regular Language Inference from Probabilistic Samples. A statistical test can be used to decide if two finite samples are drawn from the same distribution or not (and hence belong to the same stochastic set of tails). Since a number of different tests can be employed, RLIPS represents a family of algorithms, of which ALERGIA is one. ALERGIA uses the Hoeffding statistical test and Carrasco and Oncina [1999] and de la Higuera and Thollard [2000] showed that this method provably converges to the target DPFA with probability one. In other words, ALERGIA successfully learns both the structure and the transitional probabilities, and it does so with polynomial time and data.

Clark and Thollard [2004] also obtained a theoretical learning result for the class of distributions definable from DPFA, this time in a variant of the Probably Approximately Correct (PAC) framework. Kearns and Vazirani [1994] established that the class of distributions describable with DPFA is not PAC-learnable. Clark and Thollard combine the state-merging insights from ALERGIA with the insights of Ron et al. [1995], who developed a PAC-like learning algorithm for a class of acyclic DPFA. As before, the idea is to only merge states in a prefix tree if the prefixes share the same stochastic set of tails. Instead of using the Hoeffding test, however, Clark and Thollard (following Ron et al.) adopt the Kullback–Leibler Divergence as a way to measure the error between two distributions (see Section 2.2.6). Because this introduces additional parameters into the learning framework, they refer to their learning criteria as KL-PAC.

de la Higuera [2010] referred to the Clark and Thollard algorithm as DSAI for "Distinguishing Strings Automata Inference." This is because crucial to their algorithm and its analysis is the notion of "distinguishing strings" which reveal whether two states have the same stochastic tail set or not. Specifically, Clark and Thollard considered some $\mu > 0$ and define for every pair of states in a DPFA, a string w to be "μ-distinguishing" if the difference between the probability assigned to w in the stochastic tail set of one prefix and the probability assigned to w in the stochastic tail set of the other prefix is greater than μ.

Together these results show that it is possible to efficiently learn, in certain senses, both the structure and the transitional probabilities of the DPFA that model regular deterministic stochastic languages.

3.9.4   STRUCTURE OF THE CLASS IS NON-DETERMINISTIC AND NOT KNOWN A PRIORI

Methods for learning the class of non-deterministic regular stochastic languages face hurdles. Abe and Warmuth [1992] established that learning the class of non-deterministic regular stochastic languages is hard.

One clue to why this is the case might come from that the fact that although this class of distributions can be modeled with both HMMs and PFA, there are no canonical forms for the distributions in this class. Thus, unlike the classes discussed above, it is not possible for the *global* structure of the underlying grammar to be determined from a series of *local* decisions in a prefix tree. Whether or not two prefixes correspond to the same state in the underlying representation is *independent* from whether they share the same stochastic set of tails or not.

Another related reason for the difficulty is the *credit* problem. When the structure is known and deterministic, there is exactly one parse for each string in the sample and so it is clear where and how to adjust the probabilities in the transitions of the automata. However, when the unknown structure is non-deterministic, there are potentially many distinct parses of a string in the sample. In this case, it is not clear which transitions in the underlying automata are responsible and how their probabilities should be adjusted to maximize the likelihood of the sample.

Nonetheless, a number of powerful statistical methods have been, and continue to be, developed. These methods do not have the same theoretical guarantees as the algorithms mentioned above. We briefly mention two approaches.

The Expectation-Maximization algorithm offers one way to update probabilities that guarantees reaching a *local* optimum in the likelihood space. The idea is to first make an initial estimation of the number of states of a fully connected PFA and the weights on the transitions and then iterate through two steps: (1) estimating the counts obtained from the sample using the weights (expectation step) and (2) adjusting them in a way that increases the likelihood of the sample (maximization step). This approach is implemented via a dynamic programming approach known as the Baum–Welch method. Readers are referred to Jurafsky and Martin [2008] and de la Higuera [2010] for details.

A second, more recent approach is called *spectral learning*, which decomposes the target function according to its Hankel matrix, a concept borrowed from algebraic theory. For any stochastic distribution D describable with a PFA over Σ^*, the rows and columns of its Hankel matrix correspond to prefixes and suffixes, respectively, and values of cell (u, v) are assigned $D(uv)$. While this representation of D is redundant, it affords several interesting properties. The infinitely sized Hankel matrix can be partitioned into submatrices with particular properties; the number of blocks (called rank) of a particular partition relates to the size of the minimal PFA for D. Thus, spectral learning of an unknown distribution D comes down to identifying the right partition given a sample and then computing a PFA for D. Provided the rank of D is known, this is possible because the finite basis of a particular partition of the Hankel matrix ensures that only finitely many strings need to be seen in order to determine the entire Hankel matrix for D. Readers are referred to Hsu et al. [2012] and Balle et al. [2014a] for details.

The Probabilistic Automata learning Competition (PAUTOMAC) was run in 2012 as part of the biannual International Conference of Grammatical Inference. It was the first grammatical inference challenge that allowed the comparison between methods and algorithms designed to learn deterministic and non-deterministic regular stochastic languages. Challengers were provided with artificial data and tried to estimate the probabilities of unseen strings generated by the underlying probabilistic models. Results were evaluated by calculating perplexity; see Verwer et al. [2014] for details.

Perhaps one of the most striking results of the competition was put by the organizers of the competition this way: "Of course, we cannot be sure [. . .], but it seems to indicate that it is best to learn a non-deterministic model when the data is drawn from a non-deterministic distribution, and that it is best to learn a deterministic model when the data is drawn from a deterministic distribution" [Verwer et al. 2014, p. 143]. Obviously then, if we are interested in modeling natural language with stochastic grammars, we would like to know whether the underlying grammars are deterministic or non-deterministic.

3.10   SUMMARY

This chapter studied the problems of learning classes of regular languages, regular transductions, and regular stochastic languages. Different types of state-merging algorithms were shown to be able to learn different classes of these languages. The principles behind state-merging can be summarized as follows.

- Regular languages, subsequential transducers, and deterministic regular stochastic languages have canonical forms.

- Each state q in the canonical form itself represents a *residual*. For regular languages, q represents the set of good tails of strings w which lead to q. These are the set of strings which would change the state from q to a final state. For subsequential transductions and stochastic languages, the residuals are characterized similarly. In these cases the residuals are subsequential functions in the former case and stochastic languages in the latter.

- Tree representations of the sample are finite representations of the observed data. Prefix (suffix) trees distinguish each prefix (suffix) in the sample with its own state and hence its own residual.

- Criteria are used to decide when different states have the same residuals. The corresponding states are merged.

While the class of regular languages cannot be identified in the limit from positive data alone, certain subclasses of regular languages can be so identified. Rogers and Pullum [2011] and Rogers et al. [2013] discuss several natural subregular classes, some of which appear to characterize certain natural language phenomenon well.

The state-merging algorithms effectively instantiate (a priori given) inference rules. For instance, if two prefixes share a common k-long suffix then merging the corresponding states in the prefix tree will result in learning strictly $(k + 1)$-local languages. The bias selection that is undertaken in these cases can be said to be quite strong. Similarly, in the case of stochastic languages, if the deterministic structure of an underlying acceptor is known, the bias selection is very strong and learning the transitional probabilities is straightforward.

The class of regular languages can efficiently identified in the limit from positive and negative data by the algorithm RPNI. RPNI merges pairs of states provided the result is consistent with the sample of positive and negative it is given.

Similarly, the class of subsequential transductions can be efficiently identified in the limit from positive examples by OSTIA. Because subsequential transductions are functional, a positive example also provides implicit negative evidence. Consequently, OSTIA is very similar in spirit to RPNI.

Similarly again, the class of regular deterministic stochastic languages can be efficiently identified in the limit from positive examples by ALERGIA. Drawing a stochastic sample also allows for implicit negative evidence to become available. Like regular languages and subsequential transductions, regular deterministic stochastic languages admit canonical forms. ALERGIA merges states in the prefix tree provided that the residuals of those prefixes are considered to be equivalent. There are different tests available for this, but de la Higuera and Thollard [2000] showed that the Hoeffding test used by ALERGIA is theoretically sound and leads to convergence in the limit with probability 1.

The bias selection in these last three cases is also strong (deterministic regular grammars), but is considerably weaker than trying to learn *subclasses* of regular languages, functions, or stochastic regular languages. The development of algorithms that provably and efficiently learn these classes under the criteria provided are some of the key achievements of the field of grammatical inference. This is why de la Higuera [2010] presented detailed treatments of these algorithms with example runs. Readers are referred to that book for details about these algorithms that are not covered here.

As mentioned, targeting subclasses of the subsequential functions or regular deterministic stochastic languages strengthens the bias selection. Subclasses of subsequential functions have only recently been studied and appear to be learnable under stronger, more efficient learning criteria [Chandlee et al. 2014, Jardine et al. 2014]. On the other hand, subclasses of deterministic stochastic languages have been studied previously, notably n-gram models, which are the stochastic version of strictly k-local languages. However, many others remain to be studied carefully.

Furthermore, weakening the bias selection from "deterministic regular" to "non-deterministic regular" seems to lead to trouble. For instance, the theoretical guarantees for learning the larger class of non-deterministic regular stochastic languages are much weaker. In general, the true structure of the underlying automaton is not guaranteed to be discovered with these methods. Other methods which are guaranteed to identify the grammar in the limit with probability 1, such as the enumerative methods given by Angluin [1988a], are unfortunately very inefficient. Results for learning the full class of regular relations—in contrast to the subsequential functions—are also strikingly absent.

Many tasks in computational linguistics use methods that are among the most successful for learning non-deterministic regular stochastic languages. However, to our knowledge the algorithms which are among the most successful for learning deterministic regular stochastic languages (RLIPS, ALERGIA, DSAI) have not been explored. The results of the recent PAUTOMAC competition [Verwer et al. 2014] suggest that if the underlying natural language phenomenon can be described by deterministic regular stochastic languages, then these would be fruitful algorithms for computational linguists to apply.

CHAPTER 4

Learning Non-Regular Languages

Research in the field of grammatical inference deals with learnability of languages. In general, the setup is as follows. Given a family of languages, one specific language is selected and a set of sample strings is extracted. The learner now has to identify the language, from the family of languages, that was used to generate the sample strings.

Formal grammatical inference deals with the question whether specific families of languages as a whole can be identified efficiently under certain conditions. This is shown by providing formal, mathematical proofs of learnability.

While formal grammatical inference provides us with proofs of learnability, there are situations in which it is unclear what family of languages a specific grammar belongs to. For instance, consider the task of learning natural language syntax. We do not have a formal representation of the family of (formal) languages that corresponds to the family of natural languages. However, approximations of such families of languages have been made. For instance, syntax may be approximated using context-free grammars. This leads to functional descriptions, but there are valid structures that cannot be described using a context-free grammar, and context-free grammars may describe constructions that do not occur in natural languages.[1]

In contrast to formal grammatical inference, empirical grammatical inference approaches the problem of learnability of languages from a different starting point. Whereas formal grammatical inference focuses directly on families of languages, empirical grammatical inference deals with learning specific languages. Given a set of sample strings from a specific language, empirical grammatical inference aims to learn the underlying language. Additionally, if identification of the exact underlying language is not possible, an approximation should be given.

Once an empirical grammatical inference system has been developed that can learn from a set of "interesting" languages, such as natural language syntax, we can analyze the bias of the algorithm used in the system. This bias may lead to a formal description of the family of languages the system can practically learn. Given this information, we have evidence that this family of languages

---

1. The current consensus is that natural language syntax requires at least some descriptive power of context-free and with high likelihood (mildly) context-sensitive languages [Huybrechts 1984, Shieber 1985].

is learnable. A follow-up step may be to formulate a formal proof that this family of languages is indeed efficiently learnable.

Empirical grammatical inference systems can be roughly divided into three groups. This division is based on which aspects of the model are selected, or fixed, beforehand. Essentially, these groups form a sliding scale based on the amount of flexibility in the model.

First, the potential structures may be fixed completely, which means that the system should only learn the parameters in the model that belong to each structure. An example of a model that has fixed, predefined structures is an n-gram model. In n-gram models, the structure describes substrings of n symbols that can be combined to indicate which longer strings are found in the language.

Second, we can identify models that have fixed structures, similar to that of the first type of model, but the selection of the structures is more fine-grained. For instance, the structures may be based on the structure identified from (sub)trees or context-free grammar rules that have been extracted from a treebank (this requires the input to contain some information on possible structures). Once extracted, the structures remain fixed and the model can be adjusted by setting the parameters for each of the structures.

Finally, there are models that allow for the dynamic selection or creation of structures. The structures in these models are not hard-coded or predefined using external (linguistic) knowledge as is the case when the structures are extracted from a treebank. The structures can be added or removed from the model as the system sees fit. Additionally, the model may need to set parameters for each of the structures.

In the remainder of this chapter, we will provide several examples of systems that can be found on the more flexible end of the spectrum of grammatical inference models as just described. We will first introduce a principle that allows identifying regularities in the training strings. The systems we describe in this chapter are all based on this principle; some systems explicitly start from the principle, whereas others use the notion more implicitly.

4.1   SUBSTITUTABILITY

Many empirical grammatical inference systems that focus on learning context-free grammars build on a common underlying principle. However, the way the underlying principle is applied or incorporated in the learning systems is different for each system.

4.1.1   IDENTIFYING STRUCTURE

Consider the task of learning syntactic structures in natural language sentences. The system receives a set of example sentences and should output structure. A whole range of questions arises. For instance, what should this structure look like? On what basis should the structure be assigned? Should the

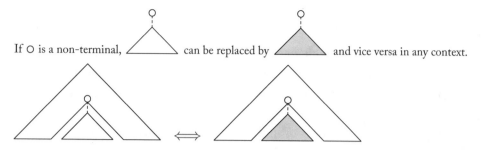

FIGURE 4.1: Substitutability in tree structures.

learned structure be what linguists would assign or should the structure at least be linguistically motivated?

If we assume that the structure assigned to the sentences should correspond to the linguistic notion of constituents[2] then we may be able to use tests for constituency to identify the structure in the sentences. There are several tests that can be used to test for constituency. Some of these tests are language specific. For instance, we may use the fact that several Germanic languages have a verb-second (V2) word order [Santorini and Kroch 2007], which means that the main verb can be found in the second position of the sentence. In this case, we may identify one or more words before the main verb, which, given the fact that the language is V2, will necessarily be a constituent.

Language-independent tests for constituency are hard to find. The most well known is that of *substitutability*. The underlying idea behind this test is that elements of the same type are substitutable. In other words, if we know that a particular group of words forms a constituent of a particular type, we may replace this constituent by any other constituent of the same type. For instance, if we know that in the sentence What is a family fare the phrase a family fare is a noun phrase, substitutability means that we can replace this phrase by any other noun phrase and end up with a syntactically correct sentence. If we also know that the payload of an African Swallow is a noun phrase, this means that What is the payload of an African Swallow is also syntactically correct.

The idea of substitutability is visualized in Figure 4.1. The type of the constituent (e.g., noun, verb phrase, etc.), indicated by the small circle, can be expanded in (at least) two ways, depicted by the triangles. The triangles represent subtrees with the words of the constituent as their yield. If one of the subtrees headed by the constituent type is found in a particular context, this subtree can be replaced by another subtree that is headed by the same type.

---

2. A constituent consists of one or more words that function as a single unit (in the context of a sentence).

Note that the notion of type in this context may be slightly different from what linguists typically describe using syntactic types. For example, in English, nouns can be preceded by determiners. However, only nouns beginning with a vowel can follow the determiner "an." For substitutability to be able to describe this phenomenon, information on the first vowel of the word should be encoded using the type, which is phonological information and arguably should not be described using syntactic types.

To formalize the concept of substitutability, we use the notion of substring. Alternative definitions can be found in van Zaanen [2002a].

Definition 4.1 (Substitutability)   Substrings u and v are *substitutable* for each other in L if given any strings l and r in Σ^*, $lur \in L \Leftrightarrow lvr \in L$

The above definition has led to theoretical work on substitutability, as for example Clark and Eyraud [2007], Clark and Yoshinaka [2014], and Scicluna and de la Higuera [2014a].

The concept of substitutability is not unlike the Nerode equivalence relation which played a central role in Chapter 3. As with Nerode equivalence, substitutability allows one to develop inference rules similar to the ones discussed in Section 3.6. There it was asked: When do we know strings u and v have the same good tails? Here, it is asked: When do we know strings u and v are substitutable?

4.1.2   LEARNING USING SUBSTITUTABILITY

The notion of substitutability does not automatically lead to systems that learn languages. The fact that constituents of the same type are substitutable only indicates the usefulness of the concept of constituency. If one knows that certain words in a sentence form a constituent of a particular type, the words may be replaced by another constituent of the same type.

Identifying constituents can be attempted by reversing the idea of substitutability. We know that constituents of the same type can be replaced, so if we can find evidence of the replacement of constituents (for instance, in several sentences), we may assume that the parts of the sentences occurring in a similar context are possibly constituents of the same type.

If we have evidence that the sentence a b c d has b c as a constituent of type X, we know there is a context a X d where X can be replaced by any constituent of type X. If we can then find other sentences that have the same context, the words on the X position in that context may indeed form a constituent of type X. For instance, if we find the sentences What is a family fare and What is the payload of an African Swallow, we may identify What is to be the context of constituents a family fare and the payload of an African Swallow, which are both of the same type (noun phrases in this case).

4.2   EMPIRICAL APPROACHES

In the last several years, a collection of empirical grammatical inference systems has been developed. In this section, we will discuss the best-known, context-free grammar learning systems. All these systems rely on some application of the notion of substitutability. Even though we try to provide a rather complete overview, there exist empirical grammatical inference systems that focus on specific properties, such as cognitive plausibility, and not simply on learning the best fitting grammar given a collection of strings. These specialized systems are not explicitly described here.

4.2.1   EXPANDING AND REDUCING APPROACHES

Even though all empirical grammatical inference systems that learn context-free grammars rely, implicitly or explicitly, on the idea of substitutability, we can identify two distinct approaches to how the complete search space is traversed. The first approach starts from the sample strings and generalizes the grammar by identifying regularities within the strings. We call this approach *expanding* as the grammar expands from a tight fit of the training data to more general grammars that capture a larger language (meaning that more strings are part of the language, even though the grammar may be smaller).

The second approach is called *reducing*. These systems start with the assumption that all strings are possible in the language. Given the valid strings in the training data, the collection of valid strings is reduced.

These two approaches are discussed in detail by van Zaanen and van Noord [2012] and are related to comparable approaches in the context of learning finite-state machines. The expanding approach corresponds to the model of the state-merging approach, whereas the reducing approach coincides with the model of the state-splitting approach.

4.2.2   SUPERVISED AND UNSUPERVISED APPROACHES

Empirical grammatical inference systems may also be grouped based on the information contained in the input. There are many possible values for this parameter.

To illustrate the parameter that indicates the amount of information, we may consider two extremes, even though, typically, these extremes do not occur in practice. On one end of the spectrum, no information whatsoever about the language is given. In this case it is extremely hard to learn, as no assumptions can be made based on the data. On the other end of the spectrum, the full information about the language is provided. This means that no learning is required at all, as everything is already known.

Typically, learners of non-regular languages receive a set of strings that are sampled from the language to be learned. This holds for all systems described in Section 4.2.4. However, alternative approaches receive other representations of the strings from the language. Examples of such representations include unlabeled tree structures, which are also called skeletons [de la Higuera 2010], partial tree structures [Sakakibara and Muramatsu 2000], or full tree structures [Charniak 1993]. We will concentrate on learners that receive data from a plain string presentation.

4.2.3   WORD-BASED AND POS-BASED APPROACHES

From a natural language point of view, a plain string presentation may mean different things. Empirical grammatical inference systems that work on real-world data, different linguistic annotation layers may serve as "plain strings." For instance, strings of morphemes, written words, or part-of-speech (POS) tags[3] as symbols in the strings lead to representations of natural language sentences. In this case, the learned grammars represent syntactic structures. Using letters or phonemes as symbols allows for the learning of morphological structure in natural language words.

The systems described below have been developed to deal with learning natural language syntax. Some systems start with tokenized (written) language in the form of words or tokens, and others are based on strings of POS tags. The major difference between these two presentations is the size of the vocabulary. Presentations consisting of strings of tokens may lead to very large vocabularies. For instance, the Google Web 1T 5-gram Version 1 corpus[4] is based on 1,024,908,267,229 words of running text. This leads to a vocabulary consisting of 13,588,391 unique words (not counting words that occur less than 200 times). In contrast, presentations resulting in strings of POS tags typically have much smaller vocabularies. The Brown tag set consists of 87 unique tags [Francis and Kučera 1982], the C5 tag set used in the CLAWS project has 61 tags [Garside et al. 1997], and the Penn Treebank tag set has 45 tags [Marcus et al. 1993]. A more fine-grained tag set is, for instance, the tag set used for the Dutch D-Coi corpus [van Eynde 2005]. This tag set consists of 320 tags (grouped in 12 main tag groups). This is still orders of magnitude smaller than the size of the vocabulary of words.

4.2.4   DESCRIPTION OF EMPIRICAL SYSTEMS

In this section, several empirical grammatical inference systems are described in some detail. All of these aim to learn context-free grammars based on unstructured strings of either tokens (words) or POS tags. Whereas the actual implementation is different in each system, the underlying approach is comparable. Each system effectively makes use of the notion of substitutability. Some systems do this explicitly, whereas others rely on the statistics of certain symbols occurring in similar contexts.

---

3. Obviously, these representations need to be learned as well before they can be used. For instance, phoneme, morpheme, and word boundaries will need to be identified from the sound signal, and POS tags already describe some syntactic information.

4. http://googleresearch.blogspot.com/2006/08/all-our-n-gram-are-belong-to-you.html

TABLE 4.1: Matrix for John walks, John sees Mary and Mary walks

	(.) walks	John (.)	(.) sees Mary	. . .	contexts
John	x		x	. . .	
walks		x		. . .	
Mary	x			. . .	
sees Mary		x		. . .	
⋮	⋮	⋮	⋮	⋱	
expressions					

EMILE

EMILE is an empirical grammatical inference system that is based on the explicit notion of substitutability. This system originates from research in the area of formal grammatical inference. Adriaans [1992] showed that shallow context-free grammars (in the shape of categorial grammars) are PAC learnable under simple distributions. Based on the theoretical research, a practical implementation has been built [Vervoort 2000, Adriaans and Vervoort 2002].

The system identifies context-free grammars that are context-separable and expression-separable. A grammar is context- or expression-separable if for each non-terminal in the grammar respectively a characteristic context or expression can be found. A context is characteristic, if it only appears with expressions of one particular type and an expression is characteristic if it only occurs within a context of a particular type. These grammars correspond to the family of shallow context-free grammars used in the formal proofs [Vervoort 2000].

EMILE starts with a collection of plain sentences (i.e., strings of words). These sentences are analyzed to identify possible expressions and contexts. All combinations of contexts and expressions are stored in a matrix containing the corresponding co-occurrence information. A co-occurrence matrix has one dimension with possible contexts and another dimension with possible expressions. Table 4.1 is part of such a matrix given example sentences John walks, John sees Mary, and Mary walks.

Analyzing the matrix, EMILE can identify characteristic expressions and context by comparing either entries in the rows or in the columns. This process is called one-dimensional clustering. In the case of the matrix of Table 4.1, it finds the cluster [John (.), {walks, sees Mary}], which is a characteristic context, as its expressions only occur in the same contexts. More complex types of clustering can be defined, such as two-dimensional clustering, which also takes contexts with ambiguous types into account [Vervoort 2000].

Given the characteristic contexts and expressions, grammar rules are created. For each expression e belonging to context T, a grammar rule $T \to e$ is introduced. Also, all occurrences of expressions e in the grammar are replaced by non-terminal T. A start symbol S is introduced and a grammar is created that makes sure all sentential contexts are reachable: $S \to T$.

Once the grammar rules are created, the same process is repeated. Due to the abstraction over the expressions in the grammar rules, new characteristic contexts and expressions can be identified, leading to deeper hierarchical grammar rules. For instance, if John and Mary are identified as expressions of type E, all occurrences of John and Mary are replaced by E. This means that sentences such as John sees Mary and Mary slaps John, become E sees E and E slaps E. In this situation, expressions sees and slaps share the same context, which was not the case in the original sentences. Based on this information, the expressions sees and slaps also receive the same type, which may again lead to further generalizations.

Originally, EMILE has been designed to show formal learnability of the family of shallow context-free languages. As such, the system is designed as an algorithm with known, formal properties. This does not necessarily mean that the algorithm leads to a practical system that can learn languages based on real-world data. The practical implementation of EMILE [Adriaans and Vervoort 2002] has a wide range of parameters; for instance, to restrict the size of the matrix or the number of comparisons made to identify the clusters. The choice of the settings of the parameters has an impact on the results of the system as well as the practical runtime and memory requirements of the system.

Alignment-Based Learning

Another system based on the idea of substitutability is Alignment-Based Learning (ABL) [van Zaanen 2000a, 2000b, 2000c, 2002a, 2003]. This system is presented as a framework consisting of a pipeline of phases. Based on the framework, a working system corresponds to selecting a specific module for each of the phases. A practically usable system is available [van Zaanen 2002b].[5]

As illustrated in Figure 4.2, ABL consists of two main phases. An optional third phase may be added. The first phase is called *alignment learning*, which generates a hypothesis space given a collection of strings. (In the implementation, an intermediate phase, called *clustering*, can be distinguished. This phase groups common non-terminals within the hypothesis space). The hypothesis space serves as the input to the second phase, *selection learning*. This phase selects the best constituents from the hypothesis space, which leads to a structured version of the input collection

---

5. http://ilk.uvt.nl/menno/research/software/abl

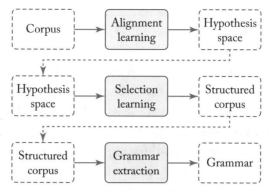

FIGURE 4.2: Schematic overview of phases in ABL.

<u>I need</u> $(_{X_1}$ a dinner during the flight$)_{X_1}$
<u>I need</u> $(_{X_1}$ to return on Tuesday$)_{X_1}$

FIGURE 4.3: Alignment of two sentences and the identification of hypotheses.

of strings. If required, a third phase, called *grammar extraction*, may be used to extract an explicit grammar from the structured output.

The system is designed to work on plain sentences, or strings of words. The alignment learning phase searches for regularities in the input. Each sentence in the training data is compared against each other sentence. Pairs of sentences are aligned, which indicates equal and unequal parts of the sentences. This is illustrated in Figure 4.3. According to the idea of substitutability, the unequal parts of the sentences are considered possible constituents, which are called *hypotheses*. Each sentence has an associated hypothesis space that contains the hypotheses for that sentence.

Each sentence is compared against all other sentences in the collection. For each of the comparisons, the alignment is done on the plain sentences. The hypotheses in the hypothesis space are not taken into account during the alignment. If hypotheses are identified, these are added to the already existing hypotheses in the hypothesis space.

The alignment of sentences can be done in different ways, each leading to a different alignment learning "module." Currently, modules using edit distance [Wagner and Fischer 1974] or suffix trees [Ukkonen 1995, Geertzen 2003, Geertzen and van Zaanen 2004] have been implemented. The edit distance–based modules align all sentences in pairs, leading to $\mathcal{O}(|C|^2)$ computation time, with $|C|$ the number of sentences in the corpus. The edit transcript of pair of sentences is used to identify the unequal parts (which consist of all edit operations except the match operation).

As an alternative to the edit distance–based modules, modules that search for words occurring in multiple sentences using suffix trees [Ukkonen 1995] have been implemented. A suffix tree is built that contains the entire collection. Branches in the suffix tree indicate positions in sentences that have the same left-hand side, but differing right-hand sides. Similarly, branches in the prefix tree (which in this context is the suffix tree from the reversed sentences) indicate positions in sentences that have the same right-hand side, but differing left-hand sides. Combining the branch points leads to the identification of equal and unequal parts in the sentences. The algorithms based on the suffix tree representation of the sentences lead to different results compared to the edit distance–based modules. The main advantage of using the suffix tree–based modules is that they can handle larger collections, as the suffix trees can be built in linear time.

Since hypotheses are added to the hypothesis space of a sentence, it may be the case that two or more hypotheses with the same opening and closing brackets are added separately. The clustering step makes sure that the non-terminals belonging to different hypotheses that share the same opening and closing brackets are merged and the different non-terminals are merged throughout the entire collection.

Adding hypotheses to the hypothesis space without taking the existing hypotheses in the hypothesis space into account may lead to overlapping hypotheses. Hypotheses overlap if the opening bracket of hypothesis x is between the opening and closing bracket of hypothesis y, while the closing bracket of hypothesis x is after the closing bracket of hypothesis y. For instance, in $(_{X_1}$ a $(_{X_2}$ b$)_{X_1}$ c$)_{X_2}$ the hypotheses of type X_1 and X_2 overlap.

Overlapping hypotheses are unwanted if the underlying grammar is considered context-free. In that case, the resulting structure after applying the phases should be seen as a tree structure, or derivation using the learned grammar. Generating sentences based on a context-free grammar leads to tree structures.

The aim of the selection learning phase is to select constituents (which are already present as hypotheses in the hypothesis space) in such a way that none of the remaining constituents overlap.

Currently, several selection learning methods have been implemented. Selection learning modules exist that select constituents chronologically or based on statistics. With the chronological selection, earlier hypotheses are considered correct, or in other words, if an alignment learning module tries to add a hypothesis to the hypothesis space that overlaps with an existing hypothesis, it is not added.

The statistics-based selection learning methods identify the most likely correct hypothesis. For each of the hypothesis, a probability is computed according to properties of the hypothesis, such as the number of occurrences of the words contained in the hypothesis. The most likely structure is then computed using a VITERBI-style optimization [Viterbi 1967].

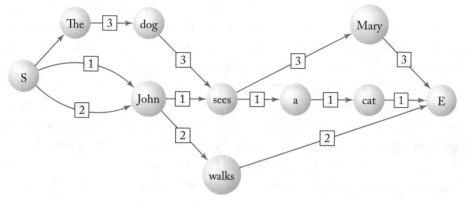

FIGURE 4.4: Initial ADIOS graph for John sees a cat, John walks, and The dog sees Mary.

ADIOS

A system that borrows ideas from finite-state automata and the notion of substitutability is called ADIOS (Automatic Distillation of Structure) [Edelman et al. 2004, Solan et al. 2005]. This system starts by representing the sample sentences from the language as a graph. The graph is compressed, which resolves non-determinism. Next, ADIOS searches for significant patterns, which correspond to substitutable parts in the sentences. These structures are considered to be constituents.

During the first phase, a directed graph (similar to a finite-state machine) is built with unique start and end nodes. For each sample sentence, a path is created. Each unique word in the sentence is represented using a node. A sentence is represented by connecting nodes with the corresponding words in the sentence. Each sentence leads to a new path, so edges are not shared between sentences. Figure 4.4 shows an example of such a graph using the sentences: John sees a cat, John walks, and The dog sees Mary.

Because nodes are shared between sentences but edges are unique for each path, words and hence parts of sentences that can be found in several sentences are automatically aligned with each other. This makes the identification of equal and unequal parts (essential information for substitutability) easy.

The second phase segments the graph by identifying subpaths that are shared by a significant number of partially aligned paths. These subpaths correspond to expressions (in a variety of contexts) which are substitutable. The subpaths are scored using the MEX (Motif Extraction) criterion. The identification of subpaths continues until no more significant paths can be found.

The MEX criterion relies on probabilities that measure changes in in- and out-degree of nodes. The changes in in- and out-degree indicate words on the boundary of substitutable expressions. For instance, a node, say, n, with a large in-degree indicates that many paths use node n. If the paths going out of node n go to many other nodes then that might indicate that node n is the end of a pattern. The idea is that a collection of paths following the same nodes indicate a subpath, or pattern, that occurs in a range of contexts. The moment the collection of paths spread out over a number of nodes, this indicates the end of the pattern.

The computation of the significant patterns is done as follows. First, probabilities are computed that measure the in- and out-degree of nodes. This computation is done separately going from left to right and right to left (indicated by P_R and P_L, respectively) to find the start and end points of significant patterns. We follow the definitions of Kunik et al. [2005].

First, we define probabilities over the out-degree of a node e_i:

$$p(e_i) = \frac{\text{\# paths leaving } e_i}{\text{total \# paths}}$$

$$p(e_j|e_i) = \frac{\text{\# paths going from } e_i \text{ to } e_j}{\text{total \# paths going out of } e_i}.$$

The relative probability of the outgoing paths can be extended to longer paths. $P_R(e_i; e_j)$ indicates the probability of the outgoing paths going from e_i to e_j:

$$P_R(e_i; e_j) = p(e_j|e_i e_{i+1} \dots e_{j-1}) = \frac{\text{\# paths from } e_i \text{ to } e_j}{\text{\# paths from } e_i \text{ to } e_{j-1}}.$$

P_R describes the probability of paths going to the right. In the same line, P_L can be defined, which describes similar probabilities, but go from right to left:

$$P_L(e_j; e_i) = p(e_i|e_{i+1} e_{i+2} \dots e_j) = \frac{\text{\# paths from } e_j \text{ to } e_i}{\text{\# paths from } e_j \text{ to } e_{i+1}}.$$

Essentially, P_R and P_L are normalized in- and out-degrees. The interesting nodes in the graph display a drop in probability when moving through the graph. This drop is measured by D, which describes the relative change of the probability between two nodes:

$$D_R(e_i; e_j) = \frac{P_R(e_i; e_j)}{P_R(e_i; e_{j-1})}$$

$$D_L(e_j; e_i) = \frac{P_R(e_j; e_i)}{P_R(e_j; e_{i+1})}.$$

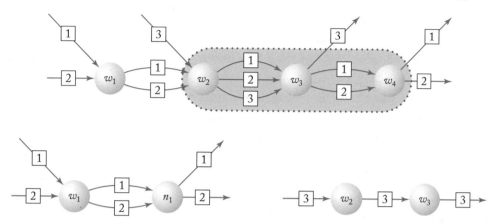

FIGURE 4.5: Above, the initial ADIOS graph. Below, the two graphs after rewriting the pattern of nodes w_2, w_3, w_4 (indicated by the dotted line in the initial graph) as node n_1.

To decide when a node may serve as the starting point or ending point of a pattern, a parameter η is introduced. If $D_R(e_i; e_j) < \eta$, e_{j-1} is used as the end of a pattern. Similarly, if $D_L(e_j; e_i) < \eta$, e_{i+1} is used as the begin of a pattern.

A problem with this approach is that the probabilities (and hence the D values) are computed based on potentially a very small number of paths going through edges. To reduce this problem, significance values are computed. This allows for an additional setting (α) that indicates a form of certainty. Typical settings for η and α are 0.9 and 0.01, respectively.

Once a start and end point of a pattern is found, a new node is created that encapsulates the nodes within the pattern. All paths going through all nodes in the pattern now go through this newly created node. For instance, in Figure 4.5, if nodes w_2, w_3, and w_4 are found to be a pattern, these are replaced by a new node n_1. Essentially, node n_1 is now a hierarchical node, as it contains nodes w_2, w_3, and w_4. Note that when paths do not go through all nodes of a pattern, these paths are retained separately. Path 3 is such an example in Figure 4.5.

CCM and DMV

The Constituent-Context Model (CCM) and Dependency Model with Valence (DMV) are two different models that both focus on different aspects of syntactic structure [Klein 2004, 2005]. By combining the results of both models, results improve. We will discuss the CCM model first, followed by DMV and finally, briefly, the combination of the two models.

CCM. CCM [Klein and Manning 2002, 2005] builds on the idea of substitutability. The aim is to identify expressions, which are called spans in CCM, in contexts. Instead of strict decisions on whether spans are constituents (as in EMILE) or hypotheses (as in ABL), CCM assigns a measure of likelihood to each span. This probability is defined as $P_{\text{span}}(s|t)$ where s is the span, i.e., a string of part-of-speech tags, and t either has the value "constituent" or "distituent" indicating whether the span is a constituent or not.

Similarly to the definition of the probability of a span, CCM defines the probability of a context c as $P_{\text{context}}(c|t)$. In this case, t (which is again either "constituent" or "distituent") describes whether the expression contained in the context is a constituent or a distituent.

The probabilities for spans and contexts are used to define the probability of a bracketing B on a string s, $P(s, B)$. A bracketing corresponds to a tree structure defined over the string. CCM starts with a uniform distribution P_{bin} over all bracketings that correspond to binary tree structures. This probability is defined as

$$P(s, B) = P_{\text{bin}}(B)P(s|B).$$

$P(s|B)$ can be expanded as

$$P(s|B) = \Pi_{i,j:i \leq j} P_{\text{span}}(s_{ij}|B_{ij}) P_{\text{context}}(s_{i-1}, s_j|B_{ij}),$$

where s_{ij} is the span over the substring of symbols starting at position i and ending, not including, at position j. The context (s_{i-1}, s_j) consists of the symbol before the start of the span (i.e., s_{i-1} which is before s_{ij}) and the symbol following the span s_j. To make sure a context can be defined when the span starts at the beginning of a string or ends at the end of a string, specific sentence boundary markers are added at the begin and end of the sentence. B_{ij} has the value "constituent" if the span over i and j is in the bracketing B and "distituent" otherwise.

Next, the probabilities are re-estimated using the Expectation-Maximization (EM) algorithm [Dempster et al. 1977]. The variables that need to be estimated (Θ) are the probabilities $P_{\text{span}}(s|t)$ and $P_{\text{context}}(c|t)$ and also the probability of the bracketing $P(B)$. In CCM, the probability of the bracketing is not changed. It is set beforehand using the uniform distribution over all binary bracketings.

The EM algorithm consists of two steps. The E step computes the likelihoods of $P(B|s, \Theta)$ given the current values of the parameters in Θ. The M step searches for new settings of the parameters Θ' that maximizes $\Sigma_B P(B|s, \Theta) \log P(B, s|\Theta')$. The EM algorithm iterates over these two steps until the values of the parameters converge.

To start the EM process, initial values for $P(B|s, \Theta)$ are needed. Klein and Manning [2005] indicated that using the uniform distribution over the binary trees has the problem that the trees are all balanced. To allow unbalanced trees to be identified during the EM process, binary trees are build

Root

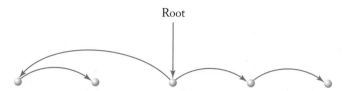

FIGURE 4.6: Example dependency parse without terminals, which are visualized as dots.

to the left and right side of a randomly chosen split point. This yields a distribution P_{split}, which has a preference for somewhat unbalanced trees.

DMV. The Dependency Model with Valence (DMV) is an unsupervised dependency parser [Klein 2004]. Instead of a one-to-many mapping between non-terminals (on the left-hand side) and terminals or non-terminals (on the right-hand side) in, for instance, context-free grammars, dependency models are a one-to-one mapping. Essentially, dependencies describe head-dependent relationships between the words in a sentence. This results in directed acyclic graphs; for instance, like the one depicted in Figure 4.6.

DMV aims to learn a dependency structure starting from the ROOT position, recursively adding new structure until all words in the sentence are covered. First, the dependent of the ROOT node is selected. From this dependent, the left and right subgraphs are added in a depth-first manner. If no more dependent can be found, a STOP condition is selected.

Following the notation of Klein [2004], the task is to learn a dependency structure D. For each word h, the left and right dependents of h are defined by $deps_D(h, l)$ and $deps_D(h, r)$, respectively. The probability of the dependency structure $D(h)$, which has h as its root, can be defined as

$$P(D(h)) = \Pi_{dir \in \{l,r\}} \Pi_{a \in deps_D(h, dir)} P_{\text{stop}}(\neg \text{STOP}|h, dir, adj)$$

$$P_{\text{choose}}(a|h, dir) P(D(a))$$

$$P_{\text{stop}}(\text{STOP}|h, dir, adj).$$

Here, $P_{\text{stop}}(\text{STOP}|h, dir, adj)$ describes the probability that h has no more dependents; h is the head, dir describes the direction, and adj describes adjacency (true if in direction dir an argument has been generated). The probability of the selection of a dependent a as the dependent of h is described by $P_{\text{choose}}(a|h, dir)$, and the probability of the dependency structure that has a as its root is $P(D(a))$.

The three parameters (P_{stop}, P_{choose}, and P_{root}, which describe the probability that a specific word is pointed to by the ROOT node) are re-estimated using the EM algorithm, just like in the CCM model.

CCM and DMV. The CCM and DMV models can be combined into a new model that assigns structure based on the structure found by both systems [Klein 2004]. The probability of a tree structure in the combined system is the product of the probabilities of the separate systems.

It turns out that the combination of CCM and DMV leads to better results compared against the results of the separate systems. This illustrates that the structures identified by CCM and DMV are complementary.

This direction of research (in particular learning dependency relations) has received considerable attention the last few years. For instance, Spitkovsky [2013] described a range of systems, Headden III [2012] incorporated lexical features, and Naseem et al. [2010] used language independent rules, like language universals.

U-DOP

The U-DOP system [Bod 2006a, 2006b] relies on Data-Oriented Parsing (DOP) [Bod 1998, Bod et al. 2003] as the underlying formalism. U-DOP starts by generating all possible (binary) tree structures and uses the DOP statistical model to decide which tree structures to keep. Because U-DOP relies so much on the DOP statistical model, we will discuss DOP first.

DOP is a grammar formalism that is structurally equivalent to context-free grammars. The difference lies in the fact that the statistical model is stronger compared to stochastic context-free grammars. Instead of assigning probabilities to context-free grammar rules, DOP assigns probabilities to elementary subtrees. Context-free grammar rules form a subset of all elementary subtrees of a tree structure. Elementary subtrees are subtrees for which on all levels in the tree either none or all children are present. This includes the entire tree structure. Figure 4.7 gives an example of a tree structure (the left-most tree) and all its elementary subtrees (which includes the full tree structure).

During parsing, elementary subtrees are combined using left-most substitution. This process combines two elementary subtrees by merging the left-most non-terminal in one elementary tree and the root non-terminal of the other node. A particular property of parsing using elementary subtrees is that there may be several ways to generate the same parse (which corresponds to a tree structure over the sentence being parsed). One such way is called a derivation and the resulting structure is

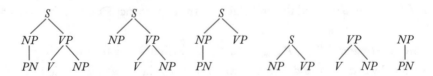

FIGURE 4.7: Elementary tree structures in DOP.

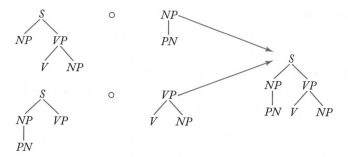

FIGURE 4.8: Two derivations using left-most substitution that lead to the same parse.

called a parse. Figure 4.8 illustrates two derivations that lead to the same parse using the elementary subtrees of Figure 4.7.

To compute the probability of a derivation, DOP follows the same principle as is used in probabilistic context-free parsing. The probability of a derivation is the product of the probabilities of the separate rules t_i (elementary subtrees in the case of DOP) being used:

$$P(t_1 \circ t_2 \circ \cdots \circ t_n) = \Pi_1^n P(t_i),$$

where $\circ$ denotes the process of combining elementary subtrees using left-most substitution (or the application of context-free grammar rules in the case of context-free parsing).

The probability of an elementary subtree is computed using the maximum likelihood estimate of a tree over all trees with the same root symbol:

$$P(t) = \frac{|t|}{\Sigma_{t':r(t')=r(t)}|t'|},$$

where $r(t)$ returns the symbol that can be found at the root of tree t. These probabilities are smoothed using Good–Turing smoothing [Good 1953].

Since there may be multiple derivations that lead to the same tree structure, the probability of a parse is computed by combining the probabilities of all derivations D that lead to the same parse T:

$$P(T) = \Sigma_{D \text{ derives } T} P(D).$$

U-DOP relies heavily on the strong statistical power of the DOP framework. The advantage of using elementary subtrees as items receiving probabilities is that in a probabilistic way, long-distance dependencies may be modeled. The disadvantage of the elementary subtrees is that given a decent size treebank, exponentially many elementary subtrees may be generated. This requires decisions, such as the use of Monte Carlo sampling [Hammersley and Handscomb 1964], to estimate the probability of a derivation to practically limit computational effort. Alternatively, one may try to reduce the exponential size of the grammar into polynomial size using PCFG reduction techniques [Goodman 1996, 2003].

U-DOP starts by generating all possible binary tree structures on a set of example sentences. Based on these structures, all elementary subtrees are generated. The probabilities of these elementary subtrees are estimated using the EM algorithm.

4.2.5   COMPARISON OF EMPIRICAL SYSTEMS

The systems that have been discussed can be compared according to different aspects. It turns out that two groups of systems can be identified. The systems within a group approach the problem in a similar way, whereas the two groups each have their own approach. Table 4.2 provides an overview of different properties of the two groups of systems. The first group consists of EMILE, ABL, and ADIOS. The second group contains CCM/DMV and U-DOP.

The first group consists of systems that start from a collection of strings of words, whereas the second group requires strings of POS tags. It has to be noted that, for instance, Klein and Manning [2002] also reported results on a dataset on which POS tags have been induced in an unsupervised way.

The systems in both groups rely on the Zipf distribution that can be found in natural language [Zipf 1929]. This distribution states that a small selection of words occurs very frequently, whereas many words only occur sporadically. In the systems that learn structure on strings of words, the frequently occurring words serve as identifiers or markers in contexts. Based on the frequently occurring contexts, expressions can be identified. The expressions consist of words that can be found in the long tail, i.e., words that only occur infrequently.

In contrast, the systems that take string of POS tags as input rely more on the probabilistic properties of frequently co-occurring symbols. These systems, which both use EM estimating to identify useful probabilities, require patterns that occur frequently enough to allow for reliable statistics. A POS tag can be seen as an equivalence class for a group of words that all serve the

TABLE 4.2: Overview of properties of the two groups of empirical systems

	Group 1	Group 2
Systems	EMILE, ABL, ADIOS	CCM/DMV, U-DOP
Input	Strings of words	Strings of POS tags
Approach	Expanding	Reducing

same (syntactic) function, such as nouns or verbs. By grouping all these words together, the problem of computing probabilities for unseen or very infrequently occurring words is reduced.

Another property in which the groups differ is the approach. The systems in group 1 slowly introduce structure only when enough evidence has been found. The reason for this is that only when useful contexts and corresponding expressions are found the systems can start identifying structure. The systems in group 2 are greedy. They start by assigning all possible structures and based on the frequently occurring structures readjust probabilities. Structures that are not useful will receive a very low probability and will not be retained.

Comparing the systems within group 1, EMILE and ADIOS are quite similar. Both systems introduce structure only when enough evidence if found (either by frequency of the context or by significant paths through the nodes). ABL always introduces structure whenever it can, but due to the greediness of the first phase, a second phase that aims to remove incorrect structure is required.

CCM and U-DOP both identify structure based on the probabilities of all possible structures. CCM is based on the context-free grammar formalism, whereas U-DOP relies on the statistically stronger DOP formalism.

4.3   ISSUES FOR EVALUATION

Formal grammatical inference results are in the form of mathematical proofs. As such, the evaluation of the work in that area is done by examining the formal proofs. The algorithms used in the proofs are typically not implemented and used on real data, but they provide evidence that a particular family of languages can be learned efficiently using the algorithm.

Empirical grammatical inference, on the other hand, starts from the notion that we know that a particular language (coming from a specific family of languages) is efficiently learnable, but a formal description of this family of languages is not necessarily or typically available. For instance, humans are able to learn languages from the family of natural languages, but we do not have a formal description of this family. Also, so far, no family of formal languages is known that can be shown to be formally learnable under any learning setting and to contain the family of natural languages.

Note that empirical grammatical inference deals with the evaluation of a learning system based on data from a specific language that is known to be a member of a family of languages. This type of evaluation does not result in (mathematical) proof of the learnability of families of languages. However, the aim is to investigate in how far a learning system can identify one or more languages. Based on this information, the algorithm itself may be investigated either to improve the results or to form the basis of formal grammatical inference proofs.

To be able to compare different empirical grammatical inference systems and to know how far away the output of a system is from the target language, an evaluation method is needed.

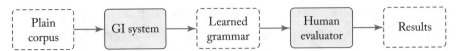

FIGURE 4.9: Schematic representation of the LOOKS-GOOD-TO-ME evaluation approach.

Several evaluation approaches are found in the literature. van Zaanen [2002a, pp. 58–62] provides an overview of three different evaluation approaches. In van Zaanen et al. [2004] a fourth approach is identified as well. Another overview of the four approaches can be found in van Zaanen and de la Higuera [2011]. We will describe each of them here in turn, together with a brief discussion of their advantages and disadvantages.

4.3.1   LOOKS-GOOD-TO-ME APPROACH

The LOOKS-GOOD-TO-ME approach is a subjective evaluation method. The approach is visualized in Figure 4.9. The grammatical inference system under consideration is applied to an unstructured collection of sequential data, a corpus. The output of the system, which can either be in the form of a grammar or a treebank version of the input data, is then evaluated manually. The person (typically the developer of the system) performing the evaluation investigates the output of the system. The evaluation may focus on specific constructions such as recursion or certain grammar rules, but it may also be a visual inspection of the entire grammar or tree structures to check for coverage. If the structures are found, the system is considered to be performing well. The evaluation is normally described in the form of textual comments.

Advantages

The LOOKS-GOOD-TO-ME approach has several advantages. First, only a collection of plain, unstructured strings is required in addition to access to an expert who can evaluate the task. This collection may be extracted from an existing dataset or the sentences may be created (semi)manually. This is particularly useful if a structured version of data suitable for the task (which would allow for alternative evaluation approaches) is not available or only small amounts can be found. In contrast, unstructured data is more often available. Natural language corpora without syntactic annotation, for instance in the form of tree structures, are more readily available than comparable treebanks. For many natural languages or linguistic domains, no treebanks are available at all.

Second, since the output of the system is analyzed by an expert, special attention may be given to specific syntactic constructions. The expert evaluator may simply disregard constructions that the system is not supposed to learn and only focus on a subset of constructions, such as the correct identification of noun phrases, or specific types of recursion.

Disadvantages

The evaluation using the LOOKS-GOOD-TO-ME approach depends heavily on the expert evaluator. Due to this influence, the LOOKS-GOOD-TO-ME approach has several disadvantages. First, the evaluator should try to provide results that are as objective as possible. However, as the evaluator is often the developer of the system, the evaluator may quickly find that the output looks good, hence the name of the approach.

Second, the comparison of multiple systems is difficult. The results of the evaluation are typically of qualitative nature. The evaluator describes the interesting aspects in natural language. This means that the evaluation of the output of several systems may still be feasible when the systems are compared in parallel at the same time, but when the outputs are compared by different experts or when the output of one system is compared with an existing evaluation, the results may be much less reliable.

Finally, if an evaluator only concentrates on the ability of a system to learn specific constructions, this evaluation only holds for those specific constructions. In other words, the evaluation is not usable as an overall evaluation of the system.

4.3.2   REBUILDING KNOWN GRAMMARS

The goal in grammatical inference is to design a system that learns a compact representation for a language given some example strings. In other words, the aim of the task is to learn a grammar. The REBUILDING KNOWN GRAMMARS evaluation approach starts from the idea that there is an underlying grammar that describes the language that needs to be learned. Given this grammar, example strings are generated, which serve as the input to the grammatical inference system. The output of the system, in the shape of a grammar, can then be compared against the original grammar. This entire process is shown in Figure 4.10.

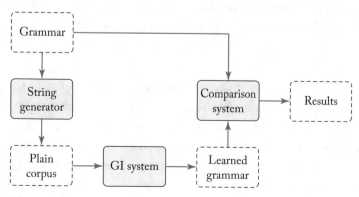

FIGURE 4.10: Schematic representation of the REBUILDING KNOWN GRAMMARS evaluation approach.

When using the REBUILDING KNOWN GRAMMARS evaluation approach, several choices have to be made. First, the actual grammar that will be used for the evaluation needs to be selected. Often, a grammar is selected from a set of well-known grammars [Cook et al. 1976, Hopcroft et al. 2001], such as the parenthesis language or Dyck language, which contains sentences consisting of balanced open and close parentheses. The results of the system on these well-known grammars illustrate how well the system works, because the results can be compared against results of previous evaluations (of other systems).

Second, a method for generating strings based on the grammar needs to be picked. Different methods for generating strings may lead to different probability distributions over the generated strings. The generative process should at the very least use all of the grammar rules at some point. However, the actual choice of how the strings are to be generated may be more complex, especially when probabilistic grammars are to be learned.

Third, the learned grammar needs to be compared against the original grammar. There are two general approaches of doing this. If the languages (i.e., the set of acceptable strings) that can be generated by the grammars are compared, the evaluation measures *weak equivalence* or *language equivalence*. If the shape of the grammar rules is taken into account as well (which comes down to comparing the tree structures generated by parsing the strings using the grammars), *strong equivalence* or *structural equivalence* is measured.

Advantages

The REBUILDING KNOWN GRAMMARS approach has several advantages. First, no sequential data is required at all, as it is generated by the grammar. This means that if a system requires more input data, this can be generated from the grammar on the fly.

Second, the influence of the evaluator is reduced (in two places). As the data is generated by an automated process, the data cannot easily be tuned to the problem. Also, the comparison of the output can be done in a more objective way, as two grammars can be compared. This leads to a more objective evaluation (compared to the LOOKS-GOOD-TO-ME approach).

Disadvantages

Even though the REBUILDING KNOWN GRAMMARS approach solves some of the problems of the LOOKS-GOOD-TO-ME approach, this approach has its own problems. First, the process that generates the training data may still influence the evaluation. As mentioned earlier, the generation process should make sure all grammar rules are used at some point, but additional requirements, such as probabilistic properties of the language (if modeled) should be considered as well.

Second, the comparison of grammars (or their languages) is problematic. With more powerful families of languages, the problem of language equivalence is undecidable. Intuitively, infinite languages require an infinite amount of comparisons before language equivalence can be established. For small grammars, humans may still be able to do a deep comparison of the grammar rules to show whether two grammars are equivalent. However, when more complex (and interesting) grammars, such as wide-coverage natural language grammars, are used, this poses problems. Note that comparing the grammars by generating strings based on one language and analyzing the generated strings with the other grammar may provide language equivalence. However, this means that a proper generation process is needed (as described above) and for more complex grammars, a large amount of strings need to be generated and analyzed.

Third, the REBUILDING KNOWN GRAMMARS approach can only be applied when the underlying grammar of a language is actually known. This is feasible with artificially created grammars, which are often used with this evaluation approach. However, this is more difficult when considering natural languages. Some wide-coverage natural language grammars exist, but the generation of training data as well as measuring equivalence of a learned grammar and the original grammar is problematic.

4.3.3   COMPARE AGAINST A TREEBANK

The COMPARE AGAINST A TREEBANK evaluation approach starts from the notion that grammars can be used to structurally annotate sentences. Instead of measuring the learned grammar (which may be difficult), this approach measures the effectiveness of learning the structure in the form of trees. The entire process is illustrated in Figure 4.11. Since van Zaanen and Adriaans [2001], this approach has been one of the main evaluation approaches in the area of empirical grammatical inference.

To perform a COMPARE AGAINST A TREEBANK evaluation, a treebank (i.e., a collection of structured sentences) is required. There are several ways to build such a treebank. For instance, the treebank may be generated from an artificial grammar. Alternatively, it may be annotated manually

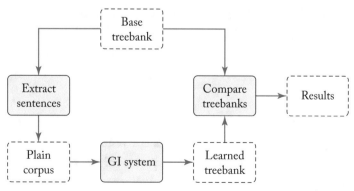

FIGURE 4.11: Schematic representation of the COMPARE AGAINST A TREEBANK evaluation approach.

or semiautomatically. This allows for the evaluation of languages for which the underlying grammar is not (fully) known.

From the treebank, the plain sentences are extracted, resulting in a plain corpus. No structural information (apart from the order in which the words occur) is present in the plain corpus. This plain corpus serves as the input to the grammatical inference system under evaluation.

The grammatical inference system is applied to the plain corpus, which results in a learned treebank. This learned treebank is a collection of tree structures. The trees are structured versions of the sentences in the plain corpus. Note that some grammatical inference systems generate a grammar and do not directly generate a treebank (whereas other systems do). If this is the case, a parser should be used to analyze the sentences from the plain corpus using the learned grammar.

The actual evaluation compares the learned treebank against the original treebank. The results of this comparison measure the degree to which the structure found in the learned treebank corresponds to the structure in the original treebank.

Several metrics exist that each measure different aspects of the two treebanks. The most well-known metrics stem from the field of information retrieval [van Rijsbergen 1979]. Precision provides a measure of the correctness of the learned structures compared against the original treebank. correct measures how many structures (which are typically described as brackets) are found in both gold (original trees) and learned collections:

$$\text{Precision} = \frac{\sum_{s \in \text{structure}} |\text{correct}(\text{gold}(s), \text{learned}(s))|}{\sum_{s \in \text{structure}} |\text{learned}(s)|}.$$

Recall measures of the degree to which all structures of the original treebank are also found in the learned treebank:

$$\text{Recall} = \frac{\sum_{s \in \text{structure}} |\text{correct}(\text{gold}(s), \text{learned}(s))|}{\sum_{s \in \text{structure}} |\text{gold}(s)|}.$$

In order to have one overall measure, the F-score is used, which is the geometric mean of precision and recall:

$$\text{F-score} = 2 * \frac{\text{Precision} * \text{Recall}}{\text{Precision} + \text{Recall}}$$

Advantages

Comparing structures from two treebanks can be done completely objectively. It is easy to evaluate another system against the same treebank and the numeric results are directly comparable.

To allow other researchers to evaluate using the same settings, standardized treebanks may be used. Using standardized treebanks also limits the possibility to tune the training data to the system (which is possible with the LOOKS-GOOD-TO-ME approach).

An advantage of this approach with respect to the REBUILDING KNOWN GRAMMARS approach is that no string generation process is required. This resolves the problem of building a dataset that measures the coverage of the entire grammar.

With respect to the LOOKS-GOOD-TO-ME approach, no language expert is required to perform the evaluation. The evaluation process can be completely automated. This also reduces the evaluation time and effort.

Disadvantages

The COMPARE AGAINST A TREEBANK approach relies on the availability of a treebank. However, such datasets are not available for a wide range of languages. This limits the possibilities of evaluation to only those languages for which such datasets have been developed.

The annotations in a treebank are performed based on a linguistic theory. Different linguistic theories lead to different types of annotation. The resulting tree structures may be quite different from the tree structures learned by the grammatical inference system. In other words, a grammatical inference system may perform well on treebanks that are annotated according to one linguistic theory, but perform badly on treebanks annotated using another theory. One of the reasons why different linguistic theories exist and are used to annotate data is that the real underlying grammar of natural language is not known.

Even though the metrics of precision and recall are well known, there are different ways of applying them to the data. Firstly, there is the difference between micro and macro recall and precision. With micro metrics, a global contingency table is constructed and used to compute the results. Macro metrics calculate precision and recall for each tree and the average of these scores lead to the overall results. Additionally, it may be unclear which structures should be taken into account. Brackets that completely cover the entire sentence or brackets that only cover one word may or may not be used (they are in a way trivial to add). These choices have a significant impact on the actual results of a system. For a proper evaluation, it has to be made clear exactly which design choices have been made.

4.3.4   LANGUAGE MEMBERSHIP

The LANGUAGE MEMBERSHIP evaluation approach concentrates on measuring whether the grammar describes the language in a weak generative sense (in contrast to COMPARE AGAINST A TREEBANK, which measures strong generative equivalence). The approach is illustrated in Figure 4.12.

Initially, the grammatical inference system is trained using the training information. The grammatical inference system tries to identify regularities within this data that allows it to decide whether newly seen sentences are either a member of the language under consideration or not.

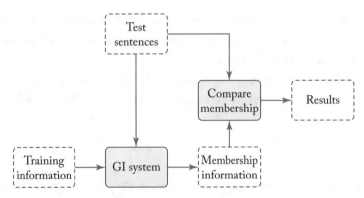

FIGURE 4.12: Schematic representation of the LANGUAGE MEMBERSHIP evaluation approach.

Next, the evaluation starts. The system is fed test sentences. This set should contain sentences that are member of the language, but also sentences that are not a member of the language to be learned. The output of the system consists of a tag for each sentence that describes whether each of the test sentences belongs to the language or not. This membership information is compared against the real language membership information, leading to the result, which describes how well the system can describe the overall language disregarding the internal structure.

Within the area of grammatical inference, this approach has been used extensively in competitions (comparable to shared tasks which are common in other areas). Examples of competitions that used this evaluation approach are Abbadingo [Lang et al. 1998], Gowachin, Omphalos [Starkie et al. 2005], and Tenjinno [Starkie et al. 2006].

Typically, this approach only measures the precision of the language membership, which is defined as the percentage of correctly tagged sentences. This means that it can measure how well the systems identify sentences belonging to the language or not, but it does not measure how well the language learned by the system covers the entire language under consideration (recall). This can only be measured properly by evaluating all sentences in the language, which is impossible in case of infinite-size languages.

Another approach to measuring coverage or recall is to generate sentences based on the learned grammar (assuming it is a generative grammar). By considering the percentage of generated sentences that is really member of the language, coverage can be measured.

If probabilistic grammars are learned, one may be more interested in how well the grammar describes the probability distribution over the sentences in the language. In this case, another metric may be more useful. Perplexity measures the probability of the test set assigned by the language model. It is defined as 2^H where H is the entropy of probability distribution P: $H = -\sum_{i=1}^{n} \frac{P(w_i) \log_2 P(w_i)}{n}$. Essentially, it measure the amount of surprise of seeing the next symbol in a string. If the probability distribution of the system (P) describes the language well, then the probability of the string will be high and hence the perplexity will be low. Another way of looking at perplexity is that lower perplexity means that a smaller number of bits is required to describe the model.

Advantages

The main advantage of the LANGUAGE MEMBERSHIP evaluation approach is that it allows for the comparison of the system disregarding the representation of the grammar. As long as the system is able to assign tags that indicate whether a sentence is member of the language or not, the evaluation may be performed. This solves, for instance, the problem of the choice of linguistic theory used in the annotation of treebanks.

Furthermore, the evaluation may be performed automatically without human interference, making this another objective evaluation method. The language under consideration may be automatically generated, but naturally occurring data (for which the underlying grammar is unknown) may be evaluated as well.

Disadvantages

A proper evaluation using this approach requires a good sentence generation method. It has to be clear that at the some point (up to infinity) in time the entire language is being tested. The choice of the method that generates test sentences may have an influence on the evaluation results. This problem also holds when recall is being measured. For this a generative grammar needs to be learned, and only using a method that is known to cover the entire grammar at some point can recall be properly measured.

When using perplexity to measure how well the learned model fits the probabilistic language, the typical approach is to evaluate the system based on the assigned probabilities per symbol. This works well for languages described by, for instance, n-gram models (which assign a probability to each symbol based on previous symbols), but for the evaluation of other types of grammars it may be necessary to measure perplexity over complete strings (and normalize over the length of the string) instead of symbols as described above.

4.4   FORMAL APPROACHES

Many of the systems described in this chapter focus on learning natural language syntax. These systems try to learn grammars that are generatively stronger than, for instance, regular languages. However, it is unclear whether the power of context-free grammars is strong enough to fully describe natural language syntax. For example, Huybrechts [1984] and Shieber [1985] indicate that some syntactic constructions may require grammars from more powerful families.

Grammatical inference research that concentrates on learning natural language syntax goes in two directions. First, empirical systems as described in previous sections aim to identify structure that corresponds to linguistic theories defined by linguists. If we can build better systems, these improvement may provide further insight into the learning process, the linguistic formalism, and (perhaps most importantly) the generative capabilities of the formal grammar formalism. Second, based on the empirical grammatical inference systems, new insights in formal grammatical inference may be gained.

Formal grammatical inference has shown that learning the family of context-free grammars is difficult, or impossible, in most learning settings. However, context-free grammars may not even be powerful enough to describe natural language syntax and some form of context-sensitive grammars may be required to do so. If learning context-free grammars is already problematic then learning context-sensitive grammars is clearly also problematic.

The solution to this problem is to identify families of languages that do not completely contain families of languages that cannot be learned efficiently. The family of natural languages may contain some context-free languages, some context-sensitive languages, but not all. In other words, it may not be necessary to have access to the full power of context-sensitiveness. In a similar line, the full power of context-freeness may not be required either.

Following this same line of thinking, there has been some research into the area of learning context-sensitive languages. For instance, Alquézar and Sanfeliu [1997] described Augmented Regular Expressions, Yoshinaka [2009] discussed variants of substitutability, and Clark [2010b] proposed Distributional Lattice Grammars. In general, however, the field of learning context-sensitive languages is still an open research area.

Another line of research in the area of formal grammatical inference, which is based on results from empirical grammatical inference, deals with formal proofs based on the approaches used in the empirical systems. In particular, the notion of substitutability has been used as the basis for the family of languages called Non-Terminally Separated (NTS) languages.

The family of NTS languages is a subset of the family of deterministic context-free grammars. An NTS grammar is defined as $G = \langle V, \Sigma, S, R \rangle$ where V is a set of non-terminals, Σ is a vocabulary, R is a set of production rules, and $S \in V$ is the start symbol. Additionally, these grammars follow the rule that for $N \in V$, if $N \stackrel{*}{\Rightarrow} \alpha\beta\gamma$ and $M \stackrel{*}{\Rightarrow} \beta$ then $N \stackrel{*}{\Rightarrow} \alpha M \gamma$. In other words, the non-terminals in the grammar correspond exactly with the notion of substitutability. The family of NTS grammars have been shown to be efficiently PAC learnable as well as identifiable in the limit [Clark and Eyraud 2005, 2007, Clark 2006].

Unfortunately, it is easy to see that natural languages are not NTS languages. There are situations in which substitutability leads to incorrect structures. For instance, if we consider the sentences John eats <u>meat</u> and John eats <u>much</u>, according to the notion of substitutability, the words meat and much belong to the same equivalence class. This means that in all cases the two words are interchangeable. However, in practice this is not the case. This example illustrates that learning based on substitutability learns a family of languages that is different from the family of natural languages.

The fields of formal and empirical grammatical inference both provide their own view on learning languages. On the one hand, formal grammatical inference shows learnability of families of languages under certain conditions. On the other hand, empirical grammatical inference shows practical possibilities and limitations of learning from real-world data. The ultimate aim of grammatical inference of natural languages is to identify a family of languages that can be proved to be learnable under realistic conditions and at the same time is powerful enough to fit the family of natural languages.

4.5   SUMMARY

In this chapter, we primarily focused on empirical approaches to grammatical inference. Even though empirical approaches do not lead to formal proofs of (efficient) learnability, there are situations in which the underlying family of languages is (not yet) known. For instance, when aiming to learn natural language syntax, there is still an ongoing discussion on the required generative power.

The empirical grammatical inference approaches that we have investigated here all rely on a similar principle, that of substitutability. This principle corresponds with (linguistic) tests for constituency. By identifying parts in the set of example strings that can be substituted for each other, the learners aim to identify substrings that correspond to the linguistic notion of constituents.

Several practical systems have been treated in some detail and a comparison of these systems has been made. The systems differ in their use of the notion of substitutability. EMILE, ADIOS, and ABL directly identify substitutable substrings, whereas CCM and U-DOP both implicitly use the notion in their statistical models. Based on this comparison, the systems have been grouped into expanding and reducing approaches. These groups correspond broadly with the model-merging and model-splitting approaches, respectively, used in learning finite-state machines.

The main problem with empirical grammatical inference systems is that they are used to provide evidence for the learnability of certain languages. However, the required language family is (typically) not know beforehand, which means that the performance of the systems may not be perfect. This requires a different type of evaluation. We cannot rely on the fact that a language is learned perfectly or even within certain limits. We do like to know which systems perform better than others and we would also like to have an idea of how far away from the target we are. To measure the performance of the systems, several evaluation approaches have been used. Each approach has its own advantages and disadvantages.

Even though this chapter mainly focused on empirical systems, the ideas that underlie these systems have led to formal learnability proofs as well.

CHAPTER 5

Lessons Learned
and Open Problems

We conclude the book with a brief summary of what has been covered, the main lessons we wish to impart, and the open problems where research efforts ought to be directed.

5.1 SUMMARY

In Chapter 1, learning problems were introduced from the perspective of theoretical computer science. Like other problems in computer science, it can be approached both formally and empirically, and both have an important role to play in securing new knowledge. In Chapter 2, principles of grammatical inference were explained and an overview of the formal methods and results were presented. Several different definitions of learning were introduced, and several different classes of grammars and formal languages were presented. Chapter 3 studied how linguistic generalizations which can be represented with finite-state grammars can be learned. It was explained how many formal results are based on state-merging and some a priori knowledge of the underlying finite-state structure, which can be partial (the machine is deterministic) or complete (the machine has these states and transitions). Chapter 4 studied learning problems where the targets cannot be represented with finite-state grammars. In contrast to the previous chapters, this chapter focused on empirical methods, and particular tasks. The important concept of substitutability was introduced and shown to underlie many systems that target context-free languages for learning. Different approaches to evaluating empirical learning systems were also explained.

It is not an accident that Chapter 3 focused on formal results and Chapter 4 on empirical results. Generally, there is a greater understanding of the learning problem when the targets of learning can be represented with finite-state grammars than when they cannot be. (Of course, this is not to say that there are no formal learning results for non-regular languages. As discussed in Chapter 4, the work of Alexander Clark and his colleagues over the past decade formalized and generalized important insights provided by the concept of substitutability.)

5.2 LESSONS

We hope that readers have come to appreciate that "learning" can be defined in different ways. Characterizing the learning problem is just as important as presenting solutions to it. In fact, several aspects of the learning problem need to be defined: the family of languages that the learner aims to learn (which defines the set of targets), the learning process (describing which information is provided by the oracle to the learner and how this transfer of information takes place), and the evaluation of the end result (which measures whether the learner's output counts as success).

We also hope that readers have come to appreciate the role grammatical structure plays in learning. A priori knowledge of *some* grammatical structure can really help. This a priori knowledge can be thought of as a learning bias. We have argued that this bias is present in learning systems, whether it is implicit or explicit. We believe understanding comes when it is explicit, so its consequences can be studied and evaluated carefully.

5.3 PROBLEMS

The field of grammatical inference has been around for over 40 years. Research in the field has led to a range of results. However, there are also still many open problems. de la Higuera [2006] discussed some open problems in grammatical inference. These are not necessarily linguistically motivated but may be of interest to the more theoretically oriented reader. In this section, we provide a broad perspective on currently open problems.

5.3.1 LEARNING TARGETS

Researchers are still identifying classes of stochastic and non-stochastic stringsets, relations, and functions relevant to natural language. This area of research is likely to continue for the foreseeable future.

The reason is partly due to the fact that most formal results that use the families of the Chomsky Hierarchy have been negative: these families of languages are not learnable efficiently from positive data. At the same time, we also know that there are constructions, or patterns, that require the grammars of natural languages to contain relatively strong syntactic constructions [Shieber 1985], which seems to clash with the learnability results.

One solution to this problem, anticipated by Gold [1967], is to identify a family of natural languages which cross-cuts the Chomsky Hierarchy. This has the effect of limiting the learning problem to some, but not all, context-free or context-sensitive languages. Instead, families of languages should be identified that capture the subset of languages that allows us to describe those constructions and patterns that occur in the natural languages.

In this vein, here are three areas we perceive as fruitful. We describe these areas in theoretical terms, but we stress that progress on these problems can be pursued both theoretically and empirically.

Subregular formal languages and transductions. Chapter 3 mentioned several subregular classes of formal languages that appear relevant to natural language. While some of this work was done over 40 years ago [McNaughton and Papert 1971], it has not really been noticed by the computational linguistics community, with some exceptions [Heinz et al. 2011]. Furthermore, very little of this work has been generalized to transductions (one exception is Chandlee et al. [2014]). It is expected that further research in this area will lead to a better understanding and better systems that learn certain aspects of natural language phenomena, such as phonology.

Sub-mildly context-sensitive formal languages. Chapter 4 studied the problem of learning context-free languages. Shieber [1985] has argued that there are natural languages that go beyond the context-free boundary. Several linguistic formalisms are known to generate languages which are mildly context sensitive (MCS), including Tree-Adjoining Grammars [Joshi 1985, Vijay Shanker and Weir 1994] and Minimalist Grammars [Michaelis 1998, Stabler 2011]. There seems to be no feasible way to learn the entire class of MCS languages under a variety of learning criteria, but subclasses can be so learned [Becerra Bonache et al. 2010, Clark and Yoshinaka 2014]. While these results are formal in nature, both formal and empirical results on learning sub-MCS languages is one of the cutting-edges of grammatical inference that has the potential to revolutionize our understanding of the kinds of computations present in natural language systems.

Subregular tree languages and transductions. There is another interesting approach which can be pursued which combines elements of the two above. Formal languages are sets of strings and grammars can be said to generate or recognize these sets. However, when it comes to natural languages, we are also interested in tree structures. Work in theoretical computer science has studied sets of *trees* and grammars which generate or recognize *these* sets (for an overview see Rozenberg and Salomaa [1997]). An early result established that yields of regular tree languages coincide with context-free languages [Thatcher 1967]. Much later it was realized that in fact the context-free languages are exactly the yields of the strictly 2-local subclass of regular tree languages [Rogers 1994, 1997] (cf. DOP in Chapter 4). Thus, while regular tree languages properly include strictly 2-local tree languages, the yields are the same. Regular tree transductions of regular tree languages allows one to move beyond context-free string languages. In fact, the yield of the image of a regular tree language under a regular tree transduction can yield a MCS language [Morawietz 2003, Mönnich 2006, Kobele et al. 2007,

Graf 2013]. In other words, the study and learning of sub-MCS classes of string languages can proceed by studying and learning subregular classes of tree languages and tree transductions.

An additional issue relates to the fact that most current formal descriptions of a language are rather clear-cut. Either a string is in the language or it is not. While many sentences and words in natural languages clearly belong (or not), there are situations in which it is not clear (to humans) whether the sentence or word is really part of the language or not. For instance, deep center embedding makes sentences harder to judge as acceptable. The phrase The bike that a woman rides is acceptable, but The bike that a woman that a child likes rides is harder to understand. Teasing apart issues of linguistic performance from linguistic competence is not straightforward, although guidelines do exist [Schütze 1996]. To resolve this issue, or at least to be able to describe intermediate acceptability or grammaticality judgments, stochastic grammars may be used. However, they face one significant hurdle: longer strings are eventually going to be worse (less probable) than shorter strings. While some ideas exist to address this issue [Clark and Lappin 2011, Clark et al. 2013], much remains to be done.

One very simple argument in favor of learning stochastic grammars is the fact that "absence of information is information." When attempting to learn a grammar from a large corpus, should we use the fact that the string *the* is absent, or should we only rely on those strings which are present? Stochastic grammars allow us to determine that an event with frequency 0 does not exist, and decisions can be made based on this information.

Finally, no research has yet been performed in the area of formally modeling second language learning or learning dialects. In these situations, there might be (partial) overlap or interaction between the first language and the second language.

5.3.2   LEARNING CRITERIA

The previous section identified one way of better characterizing the learning problem for natural language in terms of better characterizing the targets of learning. In this section, we discuss open areas of research that aim to better characterize the learning problem in terms of better characterizing the learning criteria itself.

The input to learning. Much work in grammatical inference characterizes the input to the learner in terms of a sequence or set of positive data, usually strings.

However, there is still an ongoing discussion on the nature of the interaction between human oracles and learners, and how much interaction or linguistic data is really accessible to the learner. In order to develop new models of active and interactive learning that describe learning settings or oracle–learner interaction more accurately, it would seem that information from linguists and the language acquisition is essential.

For instance, it seems reasonable to assume that children also have access to some aspect of the *meaning* of the sentences they hear. In other words, the input to learning is not only some linear string of morphemes or sounds, but it is that plus some semantic representation [Angluin and Becerra-Bonache 2008, Kwiatkowksi et al. 2010, 2012]. Other types of potentially useful information include the prosodic and intonational contours of utterances.

Finally, the problem of learning in the absence of noise is already difficult. So how about the harder problem of learning in the presence of noise? While there have been important advances in this regard [Angluin and Laird 1988], this is an area where advances can help bridge the formal and empirical methods.

Measuring efficient learning. de la Higuera [1997] presents a learning paradigm which requires learning algorithms to be efficient both in time *and in data*. The former is familiar: the time required to output a grammar must be polynomial in the size of the input. The second is less familiar but no less important: informally, the size of the input data needed for the algorithm to output the correct grammar for each language must be polynomial in the size of the grammar. Without the latter requirement, any learning algorithm can be transformed into a time-efficient one [Pitt 1989]. However, de la Higuera's paradigm makes the most sense for regular learning targets. It remains unclear how to successfully define efficient learning for non-regular targets. Past efforts to bound the number of errors or the number of mind changes are reviewed along with some more recent ideas by Eyraud et al. [2015].

What counts as successful learning. Finally, as explained in Chapter 2, there is always the question of what counts as successful learning.

In the case of formal grammatical inference, if exact learning is not required, what kinds of approximations are? Several influential ideas have been formulated, but undoubtedly many influential ideas remain to be formulated.

In the case of empirical grammatical inference, several ways of evaluating learning systems were discussed in Chapter 4. Certainly, each of these await improvements (for instance if more accurate treebanks or gold standards are developed) and other measures of evaluation can be developed.

To conclude, there is no shortage of research to be done in grammatical inference. Computational linguistics provides a rich, fertile domain with plenty of specific tasks and problems, which in turn provide a natural context for much of this research to take place.

5.4   RESOURCES

Readers interested in learning more about grammatical inference are directed to three sources. First, de la Higuera [2010] is a comprehensive and detailed monograph covering many aspects of grammatical inference. Second, there is a forthcoming collection of chapters by leading researchers on advanced topics in grammatical inference [Heinz and Sempere 2015]. Topics in that book include active learning, spectral learning, learning tree languages, and learning context-sensitive languages, among others. Third, the biannual International Conference of Grammatical Inference (ICGI) has been meeting regularly in even-numbered years. More information about this conference series, its published proceeding papers, associated challenges, and software for various algorithms, including ones discussed in this book, can be found at http://www.grammarlearning.org.

5.5   FINAL WORDS

We hope that this book has provided a broad picture of the goals and methods of grammatical inference as it relates to computational linguistics. This book has not attempted to be exhaustive, but instead to provide enough of a sufficient foundation of knowledge that allows readers to engage the literature in this area from its past and its future.

Perhaps we are dreaming, but if anyone comes to better appreciate the wonder of language and the wonder of language learning as a result of this book, it will have achieved its purpose.

The End.

Bibliography

Abe, N. and Warmuth, M. K. (1992). On the computational complexity of approximating distributions by probabilistic automata. *Machine Learning*, 9:205–260. DOI: 10.1007/BF00992677. 80

Adriaans, P., Fernau, H., and van Zaanen, M., Editors (2002). *Proceedings of the International Colloquium on Grammatical Inference (ICGI '02)*, volume 2482 of *Lecture Notes in Artificial Intelligence*. Springer-Verlag. 121, 136

Adriaans, P. and Vervoort, M. (2002). The EMILE 4.1 grammar induction toolbox. In Adriaans et al. [2002], pages 293–295. 91, 92

Adriaans, P. W. (1992). *Language Learning from a Categorial Perspective*. Ph.D. thesis, University of Amsterdam, Amsterdam, the Netherlands. 91

Akram, H. I. and de la Higuera, C. (2012). Learning probabilistic subsequential transducers from positive data. In *Proceedings of the International Conference on Agents and Artificial Intelligence (ICAART '13)*. 42

Akram, H. I., de la Higuera, C., and Eckert, C. (2012). Actively learning probabilistic subsequential transducers. In Heinz et al. [2012a], pages 19–33. 42

Allauzen, C. and Mohri, M. (2002). p-subsequentiable transducers. In *Implementation and Application of Automata, 7th International Conference (CIAA '02), Revised Papers*, volume 2608 of *Lecture Notes in Computer Science*, pages 24–34. Springer-Verlag. 39

Alquézar, R. and Sanfeliu, A. (1997). Recognition and learning of a class of context-sensitive languages described by augmented regular expressions. *Pattern Recognition*, 30(1):163–182. 112

Amengual, J. C., Benedí, J. M., Casacuberta, F., Castaño, A., Castellanos, A., Jiménez, V. M., Llorens, D., Marzal, A., Pastor, M., Prat, F., Vidal, E., and Vilar, J. M. (2001). The EuTrans-I speech translation system. *Machine Translation*, 15(1):75–103. 37

Angluin, D. (1980). Inductive inference of formal languages from positive data. *Information and Control*, 45:117–135. DOI: 10.1016/S0019-9958(80)90285-5. 52

Angluin, D. (1982). Inference of reversible languages. *Journal of the Association for Computing Machinery*, 29(3):741–765. DOI: 10.1023/A:1022860810097. 32, 59, 62, 65, 66

Angluin, D. (1987). Queries and concept learning. *Machine Learning*, 2:319–342. DOI: 10.1023/A:1007320031970. 25

Angluin, D. (1988a). Identifying languages from stochastic examples. Technical Report YALEU/DCS/RR-614, Yale University. 28, 52, 83

Angluin, D. (1988b). Learning regular sets from queries and counterexamples. *Information and Control*, 39:337–350. 32

Angluin, D. and Becerra-Bonache, L. (2008). Learning meaning before syntax. In Clark et al. [2008], pages 1–14. DOI: 10.1007/978-3-540-88009-7_1. 119

Angluin, D. and Laird, P. (1988). Learning from noisy examples. *Machine Learning*, 2:343–370. 119

Applegate, R. (1972). *Ineseño Chumash Grammar*. Ph.D. thesis, University of California, Berkeley. 76

Applegate, R. (2007). *Samala-English dictionary: A guide to the Samala language of the Ineseño Chumash People*. Santa Ynez Band of Chumash Indians. 76

Bailey, T. (1995). *Nonmetrical Constraints on Stress*. Ph.D. thesis, University of Minnesota. Ann Arbor, Michigan. Stress System Database available at http://www.cf.ac.uk/psych/ssd/index.html. 65

Bailly, R. (2011). QWA: Spectral algorithm. *Journal of Machine Learning Research - Workshop and Conference Proceedings, Proceedings of the Asian Conference on Machine Learning ACML '11*, 20:147–163. 37

Balle, B., Carreras, X., Luque, F. M., and Quattoni, A. (2014a). Spectral learning of weighted automata. *Machine Learning*, 96(1–2):33–63. DOI: 10.1007/s10994-013-5416-x. 42, 81

Balle, B., Castro, J., and Gavaldà, R. (2010). A lower bound for learning distributions generated by probabilistic automata. In *Proceedings of the International Conference on Algorithmic Learning Theory (ALT '10)*, volume 6331 of *Lecture Notes in Computer Science*, pages 179–193. Springer-Verlag. DOI: 10.1007/978-3-642-16108-7_17. 30

Balle, B., Castro, J., and Gavaldà, R. (2014b). Adaptively learning probabilistic deterministic automata from data streams. *Machine Learning*, 96(1–2):99–127. 27, 30

Baum, L. E., Petrie, T., Soules, G., and Weiss, N. (1970). A maximization technique occurring in the statistical analysis of probabilistic functions of Markov chains. *Annals of Mathematical Statistics*, 41:164–171. 37, 38

Becerra Bonache, L., Case, J., Jain, S., and Stephan, F. (2010). Iterative learning of simple external contextual languages. *Theoretical Computer Science*, 411:2741–2756. 117

Beros, A. and de la Higuera, C. (2014). A canonical semi-deterministic transducer. In Clark et al. [2014], pages 33–48. 39

Bod, R. (1998). *Beyond Grammar—An Experience-Based Theory of Language*, volume 88 of *CSLI Lecture Notes*. Center for Study of Language and Information (CSLI) Publications, Stanford, CA, USA. 100

Bod, R. (2006a). An all-subtrees approach to unsupervised parsing. In *Proceedings of the International Conference on Computational Linguistics and of the Annual Meeting of the Association for Computational Linguistics (COLING and ACL '06)*, pages 865–872. Association for Computational Linguistics. DOI: 10.3115/1220175.1220284. 100

Bod, R. (2006b). Unsupervised parsing with U-DOP. In *Proceedings of the Conference on Natural Language Learning (CoNLL '06)*, pages 85–92, Morristown, NJ, USA. Association for Computational Linguistics. DOI: 10.3115/1596276.1596293. 100

Bod, R., Sima'an, K., and Scha, R., Editors (2003). *Data Oriented Parsing*. Center for Study of Language and Information (CSLI) Publications, Stanford, CA, USA. 100, 126

Carrasco, R. C. and Oncina, J. (1994). Learning stochastic regular grammars by means of a state merging method. In Carrasco, R. C. and Oncina, J., Editors, *Proceedings of the International Colloquium on Grammatical Inference (ICGI '94)*, number 862 in Lecture Notes in Artificial Intelligence, pages 139–150. Springer-Verlag. 37, 79

Carrasco, R. C. and Oncina, J. (1999). Learning deterministic regular grammars from stochastic samples in polynomial time. *RAIRO (Theoretical Informatics and Applications)*, 33(1):1–20. 66, 79

Casacuberta, F. and de la Higuera, C. (2000). Computational complexity of problems on probabilistic grammars and transducers. In de Oliveira [2000], pages 15–24. DOI: 10.1007/978-3-540-45257-7_2. 41, 42

Castellanos, A., Vidal, E., Varó, M. A., and Oncina, J. (1998). Language understanding and subsequential transducer learning. *Computer Speech and Language*, 12:193–228. 71

Castro, J. and Gavaldà, R. (2008). Towards feasible PAC-learning of probabilistic deterministic finite automata. In Clark et al. [2008], pages 163–174. 30

Chandlee, J. (2014). *Strictly Local Phonological Processes*. Ph.D. thesis, The University of Delaware. 71

Chandlee, J., Eyraud, R., and Heinz, J. (2014). Learning strictly local subsequential functions. *Transactions of the Association for Computational Linguistics*, 2:491–503. 71, 83, 117

Charniak, E. (1993). *Statistical Language Learning*. Massachusetts Institute of Technology Press, Cambridge, MA, USA and London, UK. 90

Chomsky, N. (1956). Three models for the description of language. *IRE Transactions on Information Theory*, page 113–124. IT-2. 19, 76

Clark, A. (2006). PAC-learning unambiguous NTS languages. In Sakakibara et al. [2006], pages 59–71. DOI: 10.1007/11872436_6. 112

Clark, A. (2010a). Distributional learning of some context-free languages with a minimally adequate teacher. In Sempere, J. and García, P., Editors, *Proceedings of the International Colloquium on Grammatical Inference (ICGI '10)*, volume 6339 of *Lecture Notes in Computer Science*, pages 24–37. Springer-Verlag. DOI: 10.1007/978-3-642-15488-1_4. 45

Clark, A. (2010b). Efficient, correct, unsupervised learning of context-sensitive languages. In *Proceedings of the Conference on Natural Language Learning (CoNLL '10)*, pages 28–37, Stroudsburg, PA, USA. Association for Computational Linguistics. 112

Clark, A., Coste, F., and Miclet, L., Editors (2008). *Proceedings of the International Colloquium on Grammatical Inference (ICGI '08)*, volume 5278 of *Lecture Notes in Computer Science*. Springer-Verlag. 122, 123, 127, 128

Clark, A. and Eyraud, R. (2005). Identification in the limit of substitutable context-free languages. In Jain, S., Simon, H. U., and Tomita, E., Editors, *Proceedings of the International Conference on Algorithmic Learning Theory (ALT '05)*, volume 3734 of *Lecture Notes in Computer Science*, pages 283–296. Springer-Verlag. DOI: 10.1007/11564089_23. 112

Clark, A. and Eyraud, R. (2007). Polynomial identification in the limit of substitutable context-free languages. *Journal of Machine Learning Research*, 8:1725–1745. DOI: 10.1007/11564089_23. 67, 88, 112

Clark, A., Giorgolo, G., and Lappin, S. (2013). Statistical representation of grammaticality judgements: the limits of n-gram models. In *Proceedings of the Fourth Annual Workshop on Cognitive Modeling and Computational Linguistics (CMCL '13)*, pages 28–36, Sofia, Bulgaria. Association for Computational Linguistics. 118

Clark, A., Kanazawa, M., and Yoshinaka, R., Editors (2014). *Proceedings of the International Conference on Grammatical Inference (ICGI '14)*, volume 34 of *JMLR Proceedings*. JMLR.org. 122, 129, 133

Clark, A. and Lappin, S. (2011). *Linguistic Nativism and the Poverty of the Stimulus*. Wiley-Blackwell Press, Chichester, UK. 28, 52, 67, 75, 118

Clark, A. and Thollard, F. (2004). PAC-learnability of probabilistic deterministic finite state automata. *Journal of Machine Learning Research*, 5:473–497. 30, 37, 66, 79

Clark, A. and Yoshinaka, R. (2014). Distributional learning of parallel multiple context-free grammars. *Machine Learning*, 96(1-2):5–31. DOI: 10.1007/s10994-013-5403-2. 88, 117

Comon, H., Dauchet, M., Gilleron, R., Jacquemard, F., Lugiez, D., Tison, S., and Tommasi, M. (1997). Tree automata techniques and applications. Release October 1 2002. http://www.grappa.univ-lille3.fr/tata. 47

Cook, C. M., Rosenfeld, A., and Aronson, A. R. (1976). Grammatical inference by hill climbing. *Informational Sciences*, 10:59–80. DOI: 10.1016/S0020-0255(76)90602-2. 106

Cormen, T. H. (2013). *Algorithms Unlocked*. MIT Press. 14

Courcelle, B. and Engelfriet, J. (2012). *Graph Structure and Monadic Second-Order Logic. A Language-Theoretic Approach*. Cambridge University Press. 47

Cover, T. and Thomas, J. (1991). *Elements of Information Theory*. John Wiley and Sons, New York, NY. 21

Dempster, A., Laird, N., and Rubin, D. (1977). Maximum likelihood from incomplete data via the EM algorithm. *Journal of the Royal Statistical Society, Series B (Methodological)*, 39(1):1–38. 98

Earley, J. (1970). An efficient context-free parsing algorithm. *Communications of the Association for Computing Machinery*, 13(2):94–102. 42

Edelman, S., Solan, Z., Ruppin, E., and Horn, D. (2004). Learning syntactic constructions from raw corpora. In *Proceedings of the 29th Boston University Conference on Language Development*. 95

Edlefsen, M., Leeman, D., Myers, N., Smith, N., Visscher, M., and Wellcome, D. (2008). Deciding strictly local (SL) languages. In Breitenbucher, J., Editor, *Proceedings of the Midstates Conference for Undergraduate Research in Computer Science and Mathematics*, pages 66–73. 65

Ellis, C. (1969). *Probabilistic Languages and Automata*. Ph.D. thesis, University of Illinois, Urbana. 72

van Eynde, F. (2005). Part of speech tagging en lemmatisering van het D-COI corpus. http://odur.let .rug.nl/vannoord/Lassy/POS_manual.pdf. 90

Eyraud, R., Heinz, J., and Yoshinaka, R. (2015). Efficiency in the identification in the limit learning paradigm. In Heinz, J. and Sempere, J., Editors, *Advanced Topics in Grammatical Inference*. Springer-Verlag. To appear. 27, 69, 119

Fernau, H. (2005). Algorithms for learning regular expressions. In Jain et al. [2005], pages 297–311. DOI: 10.1007/11564089_24. 34

Francis, W. N. and Kučera, H. (1982). *Frequency Analysis of English Usage. Lexicon and Grammar*. Houghton Mifflin, Boston, USA. 90

Fu, J., Heinz, J., and Tanner, H. G. (2011). An algebraic characterization of strictly piecewise languages. In Ogihara, M. and Tarui, J., Editors, *Theory and Applications of Models of Computation*, volume 6648 of *Lecture Notes in Computer Science*, pages 252–263. Springer-Verlag. DOI: 10.1007/978-3-642-20877-5_26. 77

García, P. and Vidal, E. (1990). Inference of K-testable languages in the strict sense and applications to syntactic pattern recognition. *Pattern Analysis and Machine Intelligence*, 12(9):920–925. DOI: 10.1109/34.57687. 32, 64

García, P., Vidal, E., and Oncina, J. (1990). Learning locally testable languages in the strict sense. In *Proceedings of the Workshop on Algorithmic Learning Theory (ALT '90)*, pages 325–338. 66

Garey, M. R. and Johnson, D. S. (1979). *Computers and Intractability: A Guide to the Theory of NP-Completeness*. W. H. Freeman. 14, 52

Garside, R., Leech, G., and McEnery, A. (1997). *Corpus Annotation*. Addison Wesley Longman. 90

Geertzen, J. (2003). String alignment in grammatical inference—what suffix trees can do. Master's thesis, Tilburg University, Tilburg, the Netherlands. Available as technical report ILK-0311. 93

Geertzen, J. and van Zaanen, M. (2004). Grammatical inference using suffix trees. In Paliouras, G. and Sakakibara, Y., Editors, *Proceedings of the International Colloquium on Grammatical Inference (ICGI '04)*, volume 3264 of *Lecture Notes in Artificial Intelligence*, pages 163–174. Springer-Verlag. DOI: 10.1007/978-3-540-30195-0_15. 93

Gelfand, A. and Smith, A. (1990). Sampling-based approaches to calculating marginal densities. *Journal of the American Statistical Association*, 85(410):pp. 398–409. DOI: 10.2307/2289776. 38

Geman, S. and Johnson, M. (2004). Probability and statistics in computational linguistics, a brief review. In Johnson, M., Khudanpur, S., Ostendorf, M., and Rosenfeld, R., Editors, *Mathematical Foundations of Speech and Language Processing*, volume 138 of *The IMA Volumes in Mathematics and its Applications*, pages 1–26. Springer-Verlag. DOI: 10.1007/978-1-4419-9017-4_1. 73, 78

Gildea, D. and Jurafsky, D. (1996). Learning bias and phonological-rule induction. *Computational Linguistics*, 24(4):497–530. 71

Gleitman, L. (1990). The structural sources of verb meanings. *Language Acquisition*, 1(1):3–55. DOI: 10.1207/s15327817la0101_2. 66

Gold, E. (1967). Language identification in the limit. *Information and Control*, 10:447–474. 23, 24, 25, 52, 116

Good, I. J. (1953). The population frequencies of species and the estimation of population parameters. *Biometrika*, 40(3–4):237–264. 101

Goodman, J. (1996). Efficient algorithms for parsing the DOP model. In *Proceedings of the Conference on Empirical Methods on Natural Language Processing (EMNLP '96)*, pages 143–152. Association for Computational Linguistics. 102

Goodman, J. (2003). Efficient parsing of DOP with PCFG-reductions. In Bod et al. [2003], pages 125–146. ISBN: 1-57586-435-5. 102

Gordon, M. (2002). A factorial typology of quantity-insensitive stress. *Natural Language and Linguistic Theory*, 20(3):491–552. Additional appendices available at http://www.linguistics.ucsb.edu/faculty/gordon/pubs.html. 65

Gordon, M. (2006). *Syllable Weight: Phonetics, Phonology, Typology*. Routledge. 58

Graf, T. (2013). *Local and Transderivational Constraints in Syntax and Semantics*. Ph.D. thesis, University of California, Los Angeles. 118

Hammersley, J. M. and Handscomb, D. C. (1964). *Monte Carlo Methods*. John Wiley and Sons, New York. 101

Hansen, K. and Hansen, L. (1969). Pintupi phonology. *Oceanic Linguistics*, 8:153–170. DOI: 10.2307/3622818. 56

Hansson, G. (2010). *Consonant Harmony: Long-Distance Interaction in Phonology*. Number 145 in University of California Publications in Linguistics. University of California Press, Berkeley, CA. Available on-line (free) at eScholarship.org. 76

Hayes, B. (1995). *Metrical Stress Theory*. Chicago University Press. 56, 58

Headden III, W. P. (2012). *Unsupervised Bayesian Lexicalized Dependency Grammar Induction*. Ph.D. thesis, Brown University. 100

Heinz, J. (2007). *The Inductive Learning of Phonotactic Patterns*. Ph.D. thesis, University of California, Los Angeles. 60, 63

Heinz, J. (2008). Left-to-right and right-to-left iterative languages. In Clark et al. [2008], pages 84–97. DOI: 10.1007/978-3-540-88009-7_7. 65

Heinz, J. (2009). On the role of locality in learning stress patterns. *Phonology*, 26(2):303–351. 65

Heinz, J. (2010). Learning long-distance phonotactics. *Linguistic Inquiry*, 41(4):623–661. DOI: 10.1162/LING_a_00015. 76, 77, 78

Heinz, J. (2015). Computational theories of learning and developmental psycholinguistics. In Lidz, J., Synder, W., and Pater, J., Editors, *The Cambridge Handbook of Developmental Linguistics*. Cambridge University Press. To appear. 52

Heinz, J., de la Higuera, C., and Oates, T., Editors (2012a). *Proceedings of the International Conference on Grammatical Inference (ICGI '12)*, volume 21. Jmlr.org. 121, 128, 136

Heinz, J., Kasprzik, A., and Kötzing, T. (2012b). Learning with lattice-structured hypothesis spaces. *Theoretical Computer Science*, 457:111–127. DOI: 10.1016/j.tcs.2012.07.017. 77

Heinz, J., Rawal, C., and Tanner, H. G. (2011). Tier-based strictly local constraints for phonology. In *Proceedings of the Annual Meeting of the Association for Computational Linguistics (ACL '11).*, pages 58–64, Portland, Oregon, USA. Association for Computational Linguistics. 78, 117

Heinz, J. and Rogers, J. (2010). Estimating strictly piecewise distributions. In *Proceedings of the Annual Meeting of the Association for Computational Linguistics (ACL '10)*, pages 886–896, Uppsala, Sweden. Association for Computational Linguistics. 77

Heinz, J. and Rogers, J. (2013). Learning subregular classes of languages with factored deterministic automata. In Kornai, A. and Kuhlmann, M., Editors, *Proceedings of the Meeting on the Mathematics of Language (MoL '13)*, pages 64–71, Sofia, Bulgaria. Association for Computational Linguistics. 77

Heinz, J. and Sempere, J. M., Editors (2015). *Advanced Topics in Grammatical Inference*. Springer-Verlag. To appear. 120

de la Higuera, C. (1997). Characteristic sets for polynomial grammatical inference. *Machine Learning*, 27:125–138. DOI: 10.1023/A:1007353007695. 27, 69, 119

de la Higuera, C. (2006). Ten open problems in grammatical inference. In Sakakibara, Y., Kobayashi, S., Sato, K., Nishino, T., and Tomita, E., Editors, *Proceedings of the International Colloquium on Grammatical Inference (ICGI '06*, volume 4201 of *Lecture Notes in Artificial Intelligence*, pages 32–44. Springer-Verlag. DOI: 10.1007/11872436_4. 116

de la Higuera, C. (2010). *Grammatical Inference: Learning Automata and Grammars*. Cambridge University Press. DOI: 10.1007/s10590-011-9086-9. xx, 21, 27, 35, 67, 69, 75, 80, 81, 83, 90, 120 de la Higuera, C., Janodet, J.-C., and Tantini, F. (2008). Learning languages from bounded resources: the case of the DFA and the balls of strings. In Clark et al. [2008], pages 43–56. DOI: 10.1007/978-3-540-88009-7_4. 27

de la Higuera, C. and Oncina, J. (2002). Inferring deterministic linear languages. In Kivinen, J. and Sloan, R. H., Editors, *Proceedings of the Conference on Leaning Theory (COLT '02)*, number 2375 in Lecture Notes in Artificial Intelligence, pages 185–200. Springer-Verlag. DOI: 10.1007/3-540-45435-7_13. 43, 44

de la Higuera, C. and Oncina, J. (2003). Identification with probability one of stochastic deterministic linear languages. In Gavaldà, R., Jantke, K., and Takimoto, E., Editors, *Proceedings of the International Conference on Algorithmic Learning Theory (ALT '03)*, number 2842 in Lecture Notes in Computer Science, pages 134–148. Springer-Verlag. 44

de la Higuera, C. and Oncina, J. (2004). Learning probabilistic finite automata. In Paliouras, G. and Sakakibara, Y., Editors, *Proceedings of the International Colloquium on Grammatical Inference (ICGI '04)*, volume 3264 of *Lecture Notes in Artificial Intelligence*, pages 175–186. Springer-Verlag. 28, 30

de la Higuera, C. and Oncina, J. (2013). Computing the most probable string with a probabilistic finite state machine. In *Proceedings of the International Workshop on Finite State Methods and Natural Language Processing (FSMNLP '13)*. https://aclweb.org/anthology/W/W13/W13-1801.pdf. 41

de la Higuera, C. and Oncina, J. (2014). The most probable string: an algorithmic study. *Journal of Logic and Computation*, 24(2):311–330. DOI: 10.1093/logcom/exs049. 42

de la Higuera, C., Scicluna, J., and Nederhof, M.-J. (2014). On the computation of distances for probabilistic context-free grammars. *CoRR*, abs/1407.1513. 30

de la Higuera, C. and Thollard, F. (2000). Identication in the limit with probability one of stochastic deterministic finite automata. In de Oliveira [2000], pages 15–24. DOI: 10.1007/978-3-540-45257-7_12. 28, 79, 82

Hopcroft, J. E., Motwani, R., and Ullman, J. D. (2001). *Introduction to Automata Theory, Languages, and Computation*. Addison-Wesley Publishing Company, Reading, MA, USA. 59, 106

Horning, J. J. (1969). *A Study of Grammatical Inference*. Ph.D. thesis, Stanford University. 28, 52

Hsu, D., Kakade, S. M., and Zhang, T. (2012). A spectral algorithm for learning hidden Markov models. *Journal of Computer and System Sciences*, 78(5):1460–1480. 38, 81

Hulden, M. (2012). Treba: Efficient numerically stable EM for PFA. In Heinz et al. [2012a], pages 249–253. 37

Huybrechts, R. M. A. C. (1984). The weak adequacy of context-free phrase structure grammar. In de Haan, G. J., Trommelen, M., and Zonneveld, W., Editors, *Van periferie naar kern*, pages 81–99. Foris, Dordrecht, the Netherlands. 85, 111

Jain, S., Simon, H.-U., and Tomita, E., Editors (2005). *Proceedings of the International Conference on Algorithmic Learning Theory (ALT '05)*, volume 3734 of *Lecture Notes in Computer Science*. Springer-Verlag. 125, 132

Jardine, A., Chandlee, J., Eyraud, R., and Heinz, J. (2014). Very efficient learning of structured classes of subsequential functions from positive data. In Clark et al. [2014], pages 94–108. 71, 83

Jelinek, F. (1998). *Statistical Methods for Speech Recognition*. The MIT Press, Cambridge, Massachusetts. 35

Joshi, A. K. (1985). Tree-adjoining grammars: How much context sensitivity is required to provide reasonable structural descriptions? In Dowty, D., Karttunen, L., and Zwicky, A., Editors, *Natural Language Parsing*, pages 206–250. Cambridge University Press. DOI: 10.1017/CBO9780511597855 .007. 8, 117

Jurafsky, D. and Martin, J. (2008). *Speech and Language Processing: An Introduction to Natural Language Processing, Speech Recognition, and Computational Linguistics*. Prentice-Hall, Upper Saddle River, NJ, second edition. xix, 76, 81

Kearns, M. and Valiant, L. (1989). Cryptographic limitations on learning boolean formulae and finite automata. In *21st ACM Symposium on Theory of Computing*, pages 433–444. 30

Kearns, M. J. and Vazirani, U. (1994). *An Introduction to Computational Learning Theory*. MIT Press. 21, 30, 48, 79

Klein, D. (2004). Corpus-based induction of syntactic structure: Models of dependency and constituency. In *Proceedings of the Annual Meeting of the Association for Computational Linguistics (ACL '04)*, pages 478–485. 97, 99, 100

Klein, D. (2005). *The Unsupervised Learning of Natural Language Structure*. Ph.D. thesis, Stanford University. 97

Klein, D. and Manning, C. D. (2002). A generative constituent-context model for improved grammar induction. In *Proceedings of the Annual Meeting of the Association for Computational Linguistics (ACL '02)*, pages 128–135. Association for Computational Linguistics. 97, 102

Klein, D. and Manning, C. D. (2005). Natural language grammar induction with a generative constituent-context model. *Pattern Recognition*, 38(9):1407–1419. DOI: 10.1016/j.patcog.2004 .03.023. 97, 98

Kobele, G. M., Rétoré, C., and Salvati, S. (2007). An automata-theoretic approach to minimalism. In Rogers, J. and Kepser, S., Editors, *Model Theoretic Syntax at 10*, pages 71–80. 117

Koehn, P. (2010). *Statistical Machine Translation*. Cambridge University Press. 46

Kornai, A. (2011). Probabilistic grammars and languages. *Journal of Logic, Language, and Information*, 20:317–328. DOI: 10.1007/s10849-011-9135-z. 72

Kullback, S. and Leibler, R. A. (1951). On information and sufficiency. *Annals Mathematical Statistics*, 22(1):79–86. DOI: 10.1214/aoms/1177729694. 29

Kunik, V., Solan, Z., Edelman, S., and Horn, D. (2005). Motif extraction and protein classification. In *Proceedings of Computational Systems Bioinformatics (CSB)*, pages 80–85. 96

Kwiatkowksi, T., Zettlemoyer, L., Goldwater, S., and Steedman, M. (2010). Inducing probabilistic CCG grammars from logical form with higher-order unification. In Li and Màrquez [2010], pages 1223–1233. 119

Kwiatkowski, T., Goldwater, S., Zettlemoyer, L., and Steedman, M. (2012). A probabilistic model of syntactic and semantic acquisition from child-directed utterances and their meanings. In *Proceedings of the Conference of the European Chapter of the Association for Computational Linguistics EACL '12*, pages 234–244, Avignon, France. Association for Computational Linguistics. 119

Lang, K. J., Pearlmutter, B. A., and Price, R. A. (1998). Results of the Abbadingo One DFA learning competition and a new evidence-driven state merging algorithm. In Honavar, V. and Slutski, G., Editors, *Proceedings of the International Colloquium on Grammatical Inference (ICGI '98)*, number 1433 in Lecture Notes in Artificial Intelligence, pages 1–12. Springer-Verlag. DOI: 10.1007/BFb0054059. 110

Lari, K. and Young, S. J. (1990). The estimation of stochastic context free grammars using the inside-outside algorithm. *Computer Speech and Language*, 4:35–56. 46

Li, H. and Màrquez, L., Editors (2010). *Proceedings of the Conference on Empirical Methods on Natural Language Processing (EMNLP '10)*. Association for Computational Linguistics. 130, 131

Lombardy, S. and Sakarovitch, J. (2008). The universal automaton. In Flum, J., Grädel, E., and Wilke, T., Editors, *Logic and Automata*, volume 2 of *Texts in Logic and Games*, pages 457–504. Amsterdam University Press. 54

Lyngsø, R. B. and Pedersen, C. N. S. (2002). The consensus string problem and the complexity of comparing hidden Markov models. *Journal of Computing and System Science*, 65(3):545–569. 30

Manning, C. and Schütze, H. (1999). *Foundations of Statistical Natural Language Processing*. Cambridge, MA: MIT Press. xix

Marcus, M. P., Santorini, B., and Marcinkiewicz, M. A. (1993). Building a large annotated corpus of English: the Penn treebank. *Computational Linguistics*, 19(2):313–330. 90

McNaughton, R. and Papert, S. (1971). *Counter-Free Automata*. MIT Press. 54, 65, 66, 117

Michaelis, J. (1998). Derivational minimalism is mildly context-sensitive. In *Selected Papers from the Third International Conference on Logical Aspects of Computational Linguistics (LACL '98)*, pages 179–198, London, UK. Springer-Verlag. DOI: 10.1007/3-540-45738-0_11. 117

Miclet, L. and de la Higuera, C., Editors (1996). *Proceedings of the International Colloquium on Grammatical Inference (ICGI '96)*, number 1147 in Lecture Notes in Artificial Intelligence. Springer-Verlag. 132, 135

Mohri, M. (1997). Finite-state transducers in language and speech processing. *Computational Linguistics*, 23(3):269–311. 39, 70

Mohri, M., Pereira, F. C. N., and Riley, M. (2000). The design principles of a weighted finite-state transducer library. *Theoretical Computer Science*, 231(1):17–32. 39

Mönnich, U. (2006). Grammar morphisms. Unpublished manuscript. 117

Morawietz, F. (2003). *Two-Step Approaches to Natural Language Formalisms*. Walter de Gruyter, Berlin. 117

Muggleton, S. (1990). *Inductive Acquisition of Expert Knowledge*. Addison-Wesley. 65

Naseem, T., Chen, H., Barzilay, R., and Johnson, M. (2010). Using universal linguistic knowledge to guide grammar induction. In Li and Màrquez [2010], pages 1234–1244. 100

Nederhof, M.-J. and Satta, G. (2004). Kullback-Leibler distance between probabilistic context-free grammars and probabilistic finite automata. In *Proceedings of the International Conference on Computational Linguistics (COLING '04)*, volume 71. Association for Computational Linguistics. DOI: 10.3115/1220355.1220366. 30

Nevins, A. (2010). *Locality in Vowel Harmony*. MIT Press, Cambridge, MA. 76

Oates, T., Desai, D., and Bhat, V. (2002). Learning k-reversible context-free grammars from positive structural examples. In Sammut, C. and Hoffmann, A. G., Editors, *Proceedings of the International Conference on Machine Learning (ICML '02)*, pages 459–465. Morgan Kaufmann, San Francisco, CA. 47

Oates, T., Doshi, S., and Huang, F. (2003). Estimating maximum likelihood parameters for stochastic context-free graph grammars. In *Proceedings of the International Conference on Inductive Logic Programming ILP '03*, volume 2835 of *Lecture Notes in Computer Science*, pages 281–298. Springer-Verlag. 47

Odden, D. (1994). Adjacency parameters in phonology. *Language*, 70(2):289–330. DOI: 10.2307/415830. 76

de Oliveira, A. L., Editor (2000). *Proceedings of the International Colloquium on Grammatical Inference (ICGI '00)*, volume 1891 of *Lecture Notes in Artificial Intelligence*. Springer-Verlag. 123, 128, 133

Oncina, J. and García, P. (1992). Identifying regular languages in polynomial time. In Bunke, H., Editor, *Advances in Structural and Syntactic Pattern Recognition*, volume 5 of *Series in Machine Perception and Artificial Intelligence*, pages 99–108. World Scientific. 32

Oncina, J., García, P., and Vidal, E. (1993). Learning subsequential transducers for pattern recognition interpretation tasks. *Pattern Analysis and Machine Intelligence*, 15(5):448–458. DOI: 10.1109/34 .211465. 38, 40, 66, 68, 70

Oncina, J. and Varó, M. A. (1996). Using domain information during the learning of a subsequential transducer. In Miclet and de la Higuera [1996], pages 313–325. DOI: 10.1007/BFb0033364. 71

Palmer, N. and Goldberg, P. W. (2005). PAC-learnability of probabilistic deterministic finite state automata in terms of variation distance. In Jain et al. [2005], pages 157–170. 30

Paz, A. (1971). *Introduction to Probabilistic Automata*. Academic Press, New York. 35

Pitt, L. (1989). Inductive inference, DFAs, and computational complexity. In *Analogical and Inductive Inference*, number 397 in *Lecture Notes in Artificial Intelligence*, pages 18–44. Springer-Verlag. DOI: 10.1007/3-540-51734-0_50. 27, 69, 119

Rabiner, L. (1989). A tutorial on hidden Markov models and selected applications in speech recoginition. *Proceedings of the IEEE*, 77:257–286. DOI: 10.1109/5.18626. 21, 35

van Rijsbergen, C. J. (1979). *Information Retrieval*. University of Glasgow, Glasgow, UK, second edition. Printout. 108

Roark, B. and Sproat, R. (2007). *Computational Approaches to Syntax and Morphology*. Oxford University Press. 37

Rogers, H. (1967). *Theory of Recursive Functions and Effective Computability*. McGraw Hill Book Company. 16

Rogers, J. (1994). *Studies in the Logic of Trees with Applications to Grammatical Formalisms*. Ph.D. thesis, University of Delaware. Published as Technical Report 95-04 by the Department of Computer and Information Sciences. 117

Rogers, J. (1997). Strict LT_2 : Regular : Local : Recognizable. In Retoré, C., Editor, *Proceedings of Logical Aspects of Computational Linguistics: First International Conference (LACL '96), Selected Papers*, volume 1328 of *Lecture Notes in Artificial Intelligence*, pages 366–385. Springer-Verlag. 117

Rogers, J., Heinz, J., Bailey, G., Edlefsen, M., Visscher, M., Wellcome, D., and Wibel, S. (2010). On languages piecewise testable in the strict sense. In Ebert, C., Jäger, G., and Michaelis, J., Editors, *The Mathematics of Language*, volume 6149 of *Lecture Notes in Artificial Intelligence*, pages 255–265. Springer-Verlag. 76, 77

Rogers, J., Heinz, J., Fero, M., Hurst, J., Lambert, D., and Wibel, S. (2013). Cognitive and sub-regular complexity. In Morrill, G. and Nederhof, M.-J., Editors, *Formal Grammar*, volume 8036 of *Lecture Notes in Computer Science*, pages 90–108. Springer-Verlag. 65, 76, 77, 82

Rogers, J. and Pullum, G. (2011). Aural pattern recognition experiments and the subregular hierarchy. *Journal of Logic, Language and Information*, 20:329–342. DOI: 10.1007/s10849-011-9140-2. 65, 66, 82

Ron, D., Singer, Y., and Tishby, N. (1995). On the learnability and usage of acyclic probabilistic finite automata. In *Proceedings of the Conference on Leaning Theory (Colt '95)*, pages 31–40. 37, 79

Rose, S. and Walker, R. (2004). A typology of consonant agreement as correspondence. *Language*, 80(3):475–531. 76

Rozenberg, G. and Salomaa, A., Editors (1997). *Handbook of Formal Languages, Volume III, Beyond Language*. Springer-Verlag. 117

Sakakibara, Y. (1990). Learning context-free grammars from structural data in polynomial time. *Theoretical Computer Science*, 76:223–242. DOI: 10.1016/0304-3975(90)90017-C. 43, 45

Sakakibara, Y., Kobayashi, S., Sato, K., Nishino, T., and Tomita, E., Editors (2006). *Proceedings of the International Colloquium on Grammatical Inference (ICGI '06*, number 4201 in Lecture Notes in Artificial Intelligence. Springer-Verlag. 123, 134

Sakakibara, Y. and Muramatsu, H. (2000). Learning context-free grammars from partially structured examples. In de Oliveira [2000], pages 229–240. DOI: 10.1007/978-3-540-45257-7_19. 90

Sanjeev, A. and Boaz, B. (2009). *Computational Complexity: A Modern Approach*. Cambridge University Press, New York, NY, USA, first edition. 21

Santorini, B. and Kroch, A. (2007). *The Syntax of Natural Language: An Online Introduction using the Trees Program*. Online version. 87

Schütze, C. (1996). *The Empirical Base of Linguistics: Grammaticality Judgments and Linguistic Methodology*. University of Chicago Press. 118

Scicluna, J. and de la Higuera, C. (2014a). Grammatical inference of some probabilistic context-free grammars from positive data using minimum satisfiability. In Clark et al. [2014], pages 139–152. 88

Scicluna, J. and de la Higuera, C. (2014b). PCFG induction for unsupervised parsing and language modelling. In *Proceedings of the Conference on Empirical Methods on Natural Language Processing (EMNLP '14)*, pages 1353–1362. Association for Computational Linguistics. 46

Scott, D. and Rabin, M. (1959). Finite automata and their decision problems. *IBM Journal of Research and Development*, 5(2):114–125. 18

Seki, H., Matsumura, T., Fujii, M., and Kasami, T. (1991). On multiple context-free grammars. *Theoretical Computer Science*, 88(2):191–229. 8

Shibata, C. and Yoshinaka, R. (2014). A comparison of collapsed bayesian methods for probabilistic finite automata. *Machine Learning*, 96(1–2):155–188. 37

Shieber, S. M. (1985). Evidence against the context-freeness of natural language. *Linguistics and Philosophy*, 8(3):333–343. DOI: 10.1007/BF00630917. 19, 85, 111, 116, 117

Solan, Z., Horn, D., Ruppin, E., and Edelman, S. (2005). Unsupervised learning of natural languages. *Proceedings of the National Academy of Sciences of the United States of America*, 102(33):11629–11634. DOI: 10.1073/pnas.0409746102. 95

Spitkovsky, V. (2013). *Grammar Induction and Parsing with Dependency-and-Boundary Models*. Ph.D. thesis, Stanford University, Stanford, CA, USA. 100

Stabler, E. P. (1997). Derivational minimalism. In Retoré, C., Editor, *Logical Aspects of Computational Linguistics*, volume 1328 of *Lecture Notes in Computer Science*, pages 68–195, Berlin. Springer-Verlag. 8

Stabler, E. P. (2011). Computational perspectives on minimalism. In Boeckx, C., Editor, *Oxford Handbook of Linguistic Minimalism*. Oxford University Press. DOI: 10.1093/oxfordhb/9780199549368.013 .0027. 8, 117

Starkie, B., Coste, F., and van Zaanen, M. (2005). Progressing the state-of-the-art in grammatical inference by competition. *AI Communications*, 18(2):93–115. 110

Starkie, B., van Zaanen, M., and Estival, D. (2006). The Tenjinno machine translation competition. In Sakakibara et al. [2006], pages 214–226. DOI: 10.1007/11872436_18. 110

Stolcke, A. (1994). *Bayesian Learning of Probabilistic Language Models*. Ph.D. dissertation, University of California. 37, 65

Stolcke, A. (1995). An efficient probablistic context-free parsing algorithm that computes prefix probabilities. *Computational Linguistics*, 21(2):165–201. 46

Sudkamp, A. (2006). *Languages and Machines: An Introduction to the Theory of Computer Science*. Addison-Wesley, third edition. 21

Takada, Y. (1988). Grammatical inference for even linear languages based on control sets. *Information Processing Letters*, 28(4):193–199. 43

Thatcher, J. W. (1967). Characterizing derivation trees for context-free grammars through a generalization of finite automata theory. *Journal of Computer and System Sciences*, 1:317–322. DOI: 10.1016/S0022-0000(67)80022-9. 117

Thollard, F., Dupont, P., and de la Higuera, C. (2000). Probabilistic DFA inference using Kullback-Leibler divergence and minimality. In *Proceedings of the International Conference on Machine Learning (ICML '00)*, pages 975–982. Morgan Kaufmann, San Francisco, CA. 37

Turing, A. M. (1950). Computing machinery and intelligence. *MIND: A Quarterly Review of Psychology and Philosophy*, 59(236):433–460. 47

Ukkonen, E. (1995). On-line construction of suffix trees. *Algorithmica*, 14:249–260. DOI: 10.1007/BF01206331. 93, 94

Valiant, L. G. (1984). A theory of the learnable. *Communications of the Association for Computing Machinery*, 27(11):1134–1142. 28, 47

Vapnik, V. N. and Chervonenkis, A. Y. (1971). On the uniform convergence of relative frequencies of events to their probabilities. *Theory of Probability & Its Applications*, 16(2):264–280. DOI: 10.1137/1116025. 47

Vervoort, M. R. (2000). *Games, Walks and Grammars*. Ph.D. thesis, University of Amsterdam, Amsterdam, the Netherlands. 91

Verwer, S., Eyraud, R., and de la Higuera, C. (2014). Pautomac: A probabilistic automata and hidden Markov models learning competition. *Machine Learning*, 96(1–2):129–154. DOI: 10.1007/s10994-013-5409-9. 37, 71, 81, 83

Vidal, E., Thollard, F., de la Higuera, C., Casacuberta, F., and Carrasco, R. C. (2005). Probabilistic finite state automata – part I and II. *Pattern Analysis and Machine Intelligence*, 27(7):1013–1039. DOI: 10.1109/TPAMI.2005.147. 35, 36, 72, 75, 77, 79

Vijay Shanker, K. and Weir, D. (1994). The equivalence of four extensions of context-free grammars. *Mathematical Systems Theory*, 27:511–546. DOI: 10.1007/BF01191624. 117

Vilar, J. M. (1996). Query learning of subsequential transducers. In Miclet and de la Higuera [1996], pages 72–83. DOI: 10.1007/BFb0033343. 39, 40

Viterbi, A. (1967). Error bounds for convolutional codes and an asymptotically optimum decoding algorithm. *Institute of Electrical and Electronics Engineers Transactions on Information Theory*, 13:260–269. DOI: 10.1109/TIT.1967.1054010. 94

Wagner, R. A. and Fischer, M. J. (1974). The string-to-string correction problem. *Journal of the Association for Computing Machinery*, 21(1):168–173. 93

Walker, R. (2000). Mongolian stress, licensing, and factorial typology. ROA-172, Rutgers Optimality Archive, http://roa.rutgers.edu/. 57

Warmuth, M. (1989). Towards representation independence in PAC-learning. In Jantke, K. P., Editor, *Proceedings of AII '89*, volume 397 of *Lecture Notes in Artificial Intelligence*, pages 78–103. Springer-Verlag. DOI: 10.1007/3-540-51734-0_53. 30

Yoshinaka, R. (2009). Learning mildly context-sensitive languages with multidimensional substitutability from positive data. In Gavaldà, R., Lugosi, G., Zeugmann, T., and Zilles, S., Editors, *Proceedings of the International Conference on Algorithmic Learning Theory (ALT '09)*, volume 5809 of *Lecture Notes in Computer Science*, pages 278–292. Springer-Verlag. DOI: 10.1007/978-3-642-04414-4_24. 67, 112

Younger, D. H. (1967). Recognition and parsing of context-free languages in time n^3. *Information and Control*, 10(2):189–208. DOI: 10.1016/S0019-9958(67)80007-X. 42

van Zaanen, M. (2000a). ABL: Alignment-Based Learning. In *Proceedings of the International Conference on Computational Linguistics (COLING '00)*, pages 961–967. Association for Computational Linguistics. 92

van Zaanen, M. (2000b). Bootstrapping syntax and recursion using Alignment-Based Learning. In Langley, P., Editor, *Proceedings of the International Conference on Machine Learning (ICML '00)*, pages 1063–1070. 92

van Zaanen, M. (2000c). Learning structure using Alignment Based Learning. In Kilgarriff, A., Pearce, D., and Tiberius, C., Editors, *Proceedings of the Third Annual Doctoral Research Colloquium (CLUK)*, pages 75–82. Universities of Brighton and Sussex. 92

van Zaanen, M. (2002a). *Bootstrapping Structure into Language: Alignment-Based Learning*. Ph.D. thesis, University of Leeds, Leeds, UK. 88, 92, 104

van Zaanen, M. (2002b). Implementing Alignment-Based Learning. In Adriaans et al. [2002], pages 312–314. 92

van Zaanen, M. (2003). Theoretical and practical experiences with Alignment-Based Learning. In *Proceedings of the Australasian Language Technology Workshop*, pages 25–32. 92

van Zaanen, M. and Adriaans, P. (2001). Alignment-Based Learning versus EMILE: A comparison. In *Proceedings of the Belgian-Dutch Conference on Artificial Intelligence (BNAIC)*, pages 315–322. 107

van Zaanen, M. and de la Higuera, C. (2011). Computational language learning. In van Benthem, J. and ter Meulen, A., Editors, *Handbook of Logic and Language*, pages 765–780. Elsevier, second edition. 104

van Zaanen, M., Roberts, A., and Atwell, E. (2004). A multilingual parallel parsed corpus as gold standard for grammatical inference evaluation. In Kranias, L., Calzolari, N., Thurmair, G., Wilks, Y., Hovy, E., Magnusdottir, G., Samiotou, A., and Choukri, K., Editors, *Proceedings of the Workshop: The Amazing Utility of Parallel and Comparable Corpora*, pages 58–61. 104

van Zaanen, M. and van Noord, N. (2012). Model merging versus model splitting context-free grammar induction. In Heinz et al. [2012a], pages 224–236. 89

Zipf, G. K. (1929). Relative frequency as a determinant of phonetic change. *Harvard Studies in Classical Philology*, 40:1–95.

Author Biographies

JEFFREY HEINZ

Jeffrey Heinz received his Ph.D. from the University of California, Los Angeles in 2007, and is currently an Associate Professor at the University of Delaware. His research lies at the intersection of theoretical and mathematical linguistics, theoretical computer science, and computational learning theory, with specializations in phonology, linguistic typology, and grammatical inference. His work in these areas has appeared in the journals *Linguistic Inquiry, Phonology, Theoretical Computer Science, Topics in Cognitive Science, Transactions of the Association of Computational Linguistics*, and *Science*, among others.

His current research interests are on establishing language-theoretic, automata-theoretic, model-theoretic, and logical characterizations of subregular classes of formal languages and transductions in order to better characterize the computational nature of phonological grammars and to better understand how they can be learned.

He has served as part of the executive committee of the Association for Computational Linguistics Special Interest Group in Computational Morphology and Phonology (ACL-SIGMORPHON) since 2007. He has been a member of the steering committee of the International Community in Grammatical Inference (ICGI) since 2012. Moving forward, he would like to also support and strengthen the work of the Association for Mathematics of Language (MOL) and the Association for Logic, Language, and Information (FoLLI).

COLIN DE LA HIGUERA

Colin de la Higuera received his Ph.D. at Bordeaux University, France, in 1989. He has been an Associate Professor at the University of Montpellier, a Professor at Saint-Etienne University, and is now a Professor at Nantes University. He has been involved in a number of research themes, including algorithmics, formal language theory, and pattern recognition. His chief interest lies in grammatical inference, a field in which he has been the author of more than 50 reviewed research papers and a monograph, *Grammatical Inference: Learning Automata and Grammars*, published in 2010.

He has developed algorithms, studied learning models, and has been trying to link classical formal language frameworks with alternative ways of defining languages, inspired by linguistic considerations or techniques developed in pattern recognition.

He has been chairman of the International Community in Grammatical Inference (2002–2007) and president of the SIF: The French Informatics Society (2012–2015).

He is currently a trustee of the Knowledge for All foundation and working toward the usage of technology for an open dissemination of knowledge and education.

MENNO VAN ZAANEN

Menno van Zaanen received his Ph.D. from the University of Leeds, UK in 2002. He holds Master degrees in both computer science and linguistics. He is currently an Assistant Professor at Tilburg University, the Netherlands. His research concentrates on empirical grammatical inference and its applications. He worked and is still working on several projects dealing with structure in different modalities, multi-modal information retrieval, question answering, and symbolic machine learning for language and music. He has taught courses on a range of topics, including digital heritage, natural language processing, language and speech technology, social intelligence, and information search. He has published on several systems that deal with both clean and noisy linguistic data, such as language independent syntactic structure induction, boundaries in compounds (of different languages), spelling checkers, part-of-speech tagging of Twitter messages, and the identification of patterns in music and text.

He is a founding member of the International Community in Grammatical Inference and was chairman between 2007 and 2010. He is International Advisory Committee member of the ACL Special Interest Group on Finite-State Methods (ACL-SIGFSM), editorial board member of the CLIN journal, and Associate Editor of the *Computational Cognitive Science* journal.

Printed in the United States
by Baker & Taylor Publisher Services